The Science of *Being Lucky*:
How to Engineer Good Fortune, Consistently Catch Lucky Breaks, and Live a Charmed Life

By Peter Hollins,
Author and Researcher at petehollins.com

Table of Contents

The Science of *Being Lucky*: How to Engineer Good Fortune, Consistently Catch Lucky Breaks, and Live a Charmed Life 3

Table of Contents 5

Introduction 7

Chapter 1. Luck of the Draw 13

Chapter 2. The Illusion of Control 27

Chapter 3. As Seen on Oprah 45

Chapter 4. Coincidence and Serendipity 63

Chapter 5. Traits for Luck 81

Chapter 6. The Four Factors 95

Chapter 7. "Strategic Luck Planning" 109

Chapter 8. What About *Bad* Luck? 127

Chapter 9. Supernatural Thinking 141

Chapter 10. Luck in Science 157

Conclusion 169

Summary Guide 171

Introduction

I wish I could say this story happened to a friend, but alas, it happened to me.

If you've never been to Las Vegas, there are actually not that many things to do, in my opinion. Correction – there are many things to do, but they all fall into a few general categories. If you're into the nightlife, the scene there is unparalleled. But if you're not, like me, then mostly what there is to do is spend too much money on extravagant activities or simply lose it gambling.

I chose to engage in the latter. This was during my third trip there, so I considered myself experienced in the nuances of gambling and superstitions. After all, I had won roughly $200 my last trip to the roulette table, so I felt like I knew what I was doing.

Now, this isn't a story about me losing a fortune. Instead, it's a story about my naked lack of understanding about how some people treat the concept of good luck and attempt to bend the will of the universe to suit their needs. *So there I was*, back at the roulette table with my lucky penny in my pocket, when I sit down next to a man who smelled like a dirty laundry hamper, and that's putting it mildly.

He was dressed in a suit and his hair looked clean and non-greasy, so what was happening here? What odd situation did I find myself in at this roulette table? I must have made some sort of face in reaction to the smell, because the man apologetically smiled and told me that he was sorry for the smell, and that it was attributable to his lucky socks. He pulled up his pant legs and showed me a pair of ratty, beige socks riddled with holes, and which didn't appear to have any elastic left in them. The socks probably started as white, but became beige through years of wear and lack of washing.

Before placing our bets, the man sheepishly grinned and said, "Last washed eight years ago. Gotta keep that luck juice!"

At that moment, I suddenly knew that my good luck charms and rituals paled in comparison to what was happening in the world. I left shortly thereafter.

The Science of Luck — good luck, being lucky, and avoiding bad luck — examines humanity's curious tendency to want to feel included in what their life has in store for them. Think about it this way: Is it more comforting to have a steering wheel appear to change the car's direction, or have no steering wheel at all and suddenly you are headed straight at a wall? Whatever luck is, we want it on our side. It seemingly has the ability to create the life we want, or leave us in ruins. If we're in the right place at the right time, perhaps we'll run into that one person who can make a huge difference in our career.

And so on. The possibilities are endless.

Is luck just another word for cosmic fate and we are born with it, or is it something that is manipulated by good luck charms like unwashed socks or avoiding black cats? Is there a certain way we can act in practical terms that will make us more susceptible to better outcomes, and what we might consider better luck?

Luckily, the results are in and it's been proven that luck is a trait which can be engineered and manufactured. It has nothing to do with four leaf clovers or broken mirrors and everything to do with changing the way we imagine the concept of luck.

Is this book going to help you become luckier and lead what appears to be a semi-charmed life? If you mean that it's going to lead you to more beneficial situations in every walk of life, then yes. After all, that's really what we're after with luck, isn't it?

Chapter 1. Luck of the Draw

What is luck, and why do people want it so badly? Why do we care if black cats cross our paths, or if we are wearing our smelly yet lucky underwear while watching our favorite teams play?

We all grow up with the general idea that our actions are not the only factor at play in the outcomes of our lives — that there is some amount of random chance that's either working in our favor or against it. We call this random chance *luck*. If we're *lucky*, good things happen, and if we're *unlucky*, bad things happen.

The belief in luck has manifested itself in different ways for different cultures and traditions for as long as there has been recorded history. In Western countries, there's an old saying: "See a penny, pick it up, and all day long you'll have good luck." In Eastern countries, many times you can't enter a restaurant without catching a glimpse of a statue of a cat waving at you.

Whatever the case, the idea of having good fortune and doing everything possible to channel this ephemeral blessing is often far more valuable to people than the coins or cats themselves. Just as accumulating good luck is highly desirable, avoiding bad luck is also of significant importance in many cultures. In fact, there are countless superstitions people hold for the sole purpose of avoiding misfortune, such as skipping the 13th floor in high-rise buildings or not walking under ladders.

The only thing we know for sure about luck is that we want to have it on our side.

The Human Need for Control

Throughout history, we have developed an increasingly better understanding of our world and universe. Yet even now, many of the complexities of our day-to-day existence are so far beyond comprehension that we can only reliably predict and understand a tiny fraction of them. It doesn't matter if you're one of the world's top engineers — there are still things that would appear magical to you. We know logically that everything is a result of cause and effect, but when we are unable to actually see the underlying cause and effect in a given scenario, we have a strong tendency to find or create other explanations for why everything is the way it is. Luck is often a convenient substitute to allow us to feel more in control and less subject to the realities of chaos theory.

We are constantly seeking control, so we think if we could only know what is going to happen, then we would be able to use that knowledge to our advantage. Hence, good luck charms and rituals. This drive for control causes us to model, predict, and manage the world around us, which has led to a great deal of scientific and technological advancement over time — but it also comes at a cost. Where we find limited or no success in our ability to understand our surroundings, we *lie* to ourselves to fill in the gaps. When things don't go as we planned or hoped, we simply explain away our failures as resulting from the incompetence of others, or just plain bad luck.

A blackjack player can control their bet and whether they hit or stay, but to beat the house consistently enough to win some money, they'll need random chance to go in their favor more often than it goes against them. They'll need luck. But the act of counting cards is important to explore here: does remembering the cards that have already been used from a deck and using that data to calculate probabilities of success given the composition of remaining cards, card counters can make better-informed decisions at the black jack table.

Is it still "lucky" to win at gambling if you know the probabilities for all the cards being dealt?

At what point does luck turn into an informed decision or calculated risk based on statistics?

And luck doesn't just apply to good things happening to us; it also applies to narrowly *avoiding* bad things happening to us — instances when the danger or negative consequences were close enough to feel. For example, someone may consider themselves lucky to be alive after escaping a car crash relatively unscathed. It would be fairly jarring to realize that you could have died, and no amount of luck or lucky underwear would have saved you — it's just how random and chaotic the world can be.

Things are continuously happening to us and around us, and we often have no ability to intervene or otherwise impact the outcomes of events in our own lives. Our winning days at the casino and the near-misses driving on the interstate are due to good fortune, while the losing days and the times actual harm does come to us are a result of bad luck.

Luck, then, is simply an explanation for why good and bad things happen to us; an attribute we use to give meaning to random events.

The idea of luck is not only useful for making ourselves feel better about the chaos around us. We commonly use luck in an effort to make others feel better too, attributing our own successes to luck rather than skill to make another person feel okay about their failures. When a basketball player makes a half-court shot at the last second to win a game, it will likely be called a "lucky shot" whether the player practices half-court shots consistently or not. The other team might still feel bad about their loss, but knowing they just caught an unlucky break can alleviate their sense of responsibility for coming up short. "Bad luck" can also explain away poor performances.

All of these examples illustrate how we tend to use luck as an attribution to create false meaning in the effort of making ourselves and others feel better. Ultimately, what we can realize is that luck is not something that comes from gods or nature. It is a human creation — *a coping mechanism* — for explaining that which we can't logically or rationally explain ourselves.

Harmful Luck

If luck is predominantly used as a means of feeling better, is there really anything wrong with believing in luck? It's an interesting question, but unfortunately, it's not a simple one to answer. Sometimes, a belief in luck can have significant consequences besides just improving people's feelings.

Given the rules of cause and effect, attributing luck to the events happening to us and around us is a form of deception, sometimes of ourselves and sometimes of others. If you deny the true cause of something, you are mischaracterizing everything. As is the case with other deceptions, there are some instances where it is harmless. A Chinese good luck tradition is to eat noodles on birthdays because they are long, like one would wish their life to be. This might not have any harmful effects, nor impact their longevity in any way.

But are there ways that attributing luck to something can cause people tangible harm? Unfortunately, yes.

Whenever we are "feeling lucky," we may tend to take on extra risk unnecessarily. And when other people are included in the impact of our hopeful choices — or we encourage them to "be lucky" themselves — we can harm others through our deception. Let's take day-trader Dave for an example. Dave regularly buys and sells stocks as his primary source of income, and from all appearances, he's doing pretty well for himself.

You'd love to make a little easy money too, so you ask Dave for tips. He tells you he's "got a lucky feeling" that X Company's stock is going to surge after their Q1 sales report, so you should buy some of their stock beforehand. He must be right about these things often — how else would he have bought that new car?

It turns out Dave just read a speculative post online and didn't actually know much of anything about X Company. What's worse, he's not the only one who read that online post, so now X Company's stock has surged before the Q1 report even takes place. When the report itself comes out and is disappointing relative to that online hype, you're now out a big chunk of change. He didn't know he was using a feeling of luck as a replacement for research and knowledge, and neither did you, and now you're both out a chunk of your life's savings.

When we remove rationality and logic from our decision-making and instead rely on gut feelings and good fortune, sometimes it's going to have negative consequences. If you don't know what causes something, you can't conclude that luck is enough to understand the effects.

The "Scientific" View on Luck

Given what we now know about luck, you may not be surprised that the concept of luck is regularly at odds with a scientific understanding of the world. And in fact, scientists often describe what we call luck by another name — chance and probability.

Upon closer examination, this simple change in terminology can be uncomfortable for many people. This is because even though luck itself may not be within our control, it does at least give us a feeling of control over a world governed by random chance. And believing in luck can potentially be even more comforting for a lot of people if that belief coincides with the idea that there's always the chance to get more luck.

Nobel Prize winner and Princeton math professor John Nash is quoted in the movie *A Beautiful Mind* as saying, "I don't believe in luck, but I do believe in assigning a value to things." We can infer that the "value" John Nash is referring to is a probability that in a random scenario given the circumstances "A," the outcome will be "B," "C," or "D." Through this scientific approach, we can't predict exactly what will happen, but we can model the likelihood of each of the possible outcomes based on the information we do have.

Luck is entirely absent from this equation, replaced by chance in the form of probabilities.

To an outsider who doesn't understand or consider the probabilities of each outcome, they may consider themselves lucky if their most desirable outcomes become reality, and unlucky if not. But if the outcomes they desire are statically improbable, and in the end they don't occur, is there actually anything unlucky about that? A scientist would more than likely argue not.

Brad Watson, scientist and author of the booklet, *There Are No Coincidences — there is synchronism, design and alignment,* said that Nash was both wrong and right. Watson believes that luck is an integral part of our existence, and even went so far as to create an equation which assigns a value to luck:

Luck 100 =
[karma 4 + modesty 1] x
[desire 4 + actions 4 + abilities 4 + contribution 4 + blessings 4]

Watson leaves it up to the individual to interpret this equation, and your own feelings about luck may determine what, if anything, it means to you. However, one need only examine some of Watson's other beliefs — such as the one that he is the reincarnation of both Jesus and Albert Einstein — to get an idea of how luck and deception often go hand in hand.

Superstition

Just because luck is an attribution of random chance does not mean that we don't try to have a say in the matter. For many who believe in luck, it is not merely some inherent quality that you either benefit from or don't, but is actually something which can be influenced by our actions. The actions we take with the intention to influence luck are called superstitions.

Superstitious actions may be deliberate attempts to bring good luck to ourselves indirectly or directly. Both fans of sports and athletes who play sports are some of the most common examples of people who engage in superstitious behavior — the athletes want an edge over their opponents in any way they can get it, and the fans just want to have some impact on the outcomes they care so much about. This is where all of those "good luck charms" are so prevalent.

Quite often, we know that our superstitions are wholly irrational as we are acting them out, but we do so anyway because they make us feel good. This may not make any difference for the fans, but for athletes, anything which improves confidence can actually improve their performance.

Not all superstitions are positive, however. Many supposed influencers of luck may be accidental, like breaking a mirror or having a black cat cross your path. Still, others are more abstract — anything associated with the number 13, for example. These are common Western superstitions, but almost all cultures have their own variations.

The factor that makes a belief a superstition is its irrationality. There is no logical reason for a fan to believe that wearing the same jersey as he did when his team won the championship will actually impact the results of any future games, but he'll do it anyway because it allows him to feel like he has some control over the outcome — that he isn't a mere bystander.

A belief in luck can be beneficial or harmful, and it can supposedly be influenced either intentionally or accidentally. It goes by various different names, and we see it for countless reasons throughout our lives — always explaining or providing meaning to that which can't be controlled or understood.

Chapter 2. The Illusion of Control

In the field of personality psychology, the locus of control is defined as the strength of a person's belief that they — and not external forces beyond their control — determine the experiences and outcomes of their own life.

Jean-Paul Sartre and Sigmund Freud are two among many philosophers and psychologists who have attributed a belief in luck to a lower degree locus of control for one's life, and subsequently, an outlet for escape from personal responsibility. Believing in luck is comforting when we fail or otherwise feel dissatisfied, because the blame for all of the negative consequences can be shifted away from ourselves. In this case, we didn't need to work harder or take a different approach; all we needed was a little more good luck and we could have been successful.

I would be remiss in mentioning the concept of control over luck without talking about the **Gambler's Fallacy**. The Gambler's Fallacy is the feeling that there are predictable patterns in what are actually random sets of events.

For example, if you roll dice, you might feel that you should eventually roll a seven because it's time for it to happen. Never mind the fact that this is not statistically or probabilistically sound; you are attempting to create order in something impossible to have control over. You want to manipulate a quantity that which will supposedly change the outcome: luck.

You are also attempting to find logic and an explanation for a random series of events. There is no better illustration than how early mankind started to see entire scenes in the night sky in the form of constellations. The pattern of stars in the sky are certainly randomized, but humans have a tendency to find patterns and put things into contexts we already know.

The Gambler's Fallacy is the notion that just because X happened, Y should happen, X shouldn't happen, or X should happen again. More often than not, these events are all independent of each other, and this should guide your decision-making to be less biased.

This cognitive bias is representative of a broader phenomenon known as *apophenia*, which is the human tendency of seeing patterns and connections in random data points. This is why people see rabbits in clouds and elaborate scenes in inkblot tests. The term was coined by neurologist Klaus Conrad, who defined the tendency as an "unmotivated seeing of connections." It seems to stem from an evolutionary desire to make sense of information and understand the current environment we are in.

Apophenia likely did serve an important purpose for those who constantly had to think about their safety and security. This still applies to many of us who live outside the concrete jungles of cities and towns. If you recognize a pattern of danger, you can more easily flee, fight back, and survive. If you miss these patterns, you're going to be something's dinner. One's propensity for apophenia could literally mean the difference between life and death. For instance, you might notice leaves rustling, the birds have disappeared, and dust is rising from a nearby bush. If you fail to put together that this is a pattern of an impending attack from a jaguar, then you're dinner. It turns out seeing patterns where they may not exist can actually be a boon — though not when you are gambling. However, they can also lead to a skewed perception of reality.

Apophenia, notably, gives rise to the locus of control.

<u>What is the Locus of Control?</u>

Renowned psychologist Julian Rotter first developed the principle of locus of control in 1954, with the main consideration of his theory being people's belief that control either resides internally or externally — within yourself, or within others and external circumstances. Whether you can truly control your reality, or if it is purely subject to others.

In 1990, Rotter described the internal locus of control as "the degree to which persons expect that a reinforcement or an outcome of their behavior is contingent on their own behavior or personal characteristics." Such an expectation can have numerous benefits, including confidence and motivation to seek out information and develop skills that will enable them to better influence people and situations. This belief in their own control can also incentivize people with an internal locus of control to be highly success-oriented, or even to become politically active.

Rotter described the external locus of control as "the degree to which persons expect that the reinforcement or outcome is a function of chance, luck, or fate, is under the control of powerful others, or is simply unpredictable." This fatalistic way of viewing the world does not come without its own benefits, which include generally being more passive and accepting. If a person believes that they do not have any control over a given matter and that they should just be at peace with whatever happens, that can give them a very even-tempered approach to life.

In sum, a person with a strong internal locus of control will take responsibility for the failure and success of their actions in achieving their desired outcome, believing that their failures are due to a lack of ability, focus, or effort. A person with a mostly external locus of control, meanwhile, will be likely to attribute their successes and failures to either being lucky or unlucky. Like many other personality traits, the locus of control is not merely black and white, but rather a spectrum. Some people have an entirely internal or external locus of control, but it is more common for individuals to have a mix of both of the views.

Interestingly, it is possible for an individual's position on the locus of control spectrum to change over the course of their life. While some people's outlook might be relatively static, the general trend is for younger and elderly people to have a higher locus of control than middle-aged people who are more success-oriented during the primes of their careers.

Due to their beliefs in their own self-control and ability to influence their environments, people with a high internal locus of control see their future as being in their own hands. There is, of course, a downside to such levels of personal responsibility. When failures inevitably occur, people with an internal locus of control also accept the blame, rather than excusing the failure based on other people or circumstances.

On the contrary, people who have a high external locus of control believe that they have little or no control over events and what other people do. Some may even allow this lack of control to go even further, believing that other people actually have control over them and there is nothing that they can do besides fall in line and accept their fate.

How does luck figure into the locus of control? Well, guess who tends to possess a greater belief and even reliance upon the concept of luck? Those with an external locus of control — luck fits neatly into that description. Both luck and an external locus of control can be characterized by accepting what happens and relying on external events.

When an individual possessing a high external locus of control finds success in life, they will be more likely to express modesty, attributing their successes to luck rather than their own skill and effort. It's not false humility — they believe it could have happened to anyone, and they were just lucky to be there. On the other hand, when they experience failure, they won't feel personally responsible to the same extent as a person with a high internal locus of control. They are able to conveniently blame bad luck, so they are less likely to dwell on failure for long.

Another characteristic of having an external locus of control is the relatively lower likelihood to be proactive or even act in their best interests. When events are chaotic and complicated, they may take a step back and let things work themselves out, assuming that they wouldn't be able to make a significant difference even if they tried.

Someone with an external locus of control would be happy if you told them "good luck," whereas someone with an internal locus of control would reply, "I don't need luck!" Which are *you* more likely to say? That will likely tell you all you need to know about your locus of control and how you feel you contribute to your life's path. The more control you feel, the more responsible and accountable you feel, and thus the harder you work. It's possible this contributes to positive outcomes.

Stable vs. Fleeting Luck

Researchers from UCLA and Columbia University teamed up to take a deeper look at how people's perceptions of luck vary and the impact it has on their behavior.

They found that generally, people who have an external locus of control can be broken up into two subcategories: those who believe luck is stable, and those who view it as fleeting.

Having a stable view of luck means that you believe people are consistently either lucky or unlucky — almost as if luck itself isn't so much an external force, but rather a personality trait. If Michael wins at blackjack five trips to the casino in a row, he must be a really lucky guy.

The group who views luck as fleeting sees it as entirely external, believing that a person's luck is unpredictable and oscillates back and forth between favorable and unfavorable. Michael has been consistently lucky to win money five times in a row at the casino, so his luck is due to run out any day now.

How do these views affect people personally?

For those individuals who have an external locus of control and a view that luck is stable, research has shown that this leads to a *higher* drive for achieving personal success. This stable outlook is correlated with greater feelings of personal control, which is in turn attributable to being more motivated and proactive about achieving the outcomes they desire.

Upon closer examination, this phenomenon makes sense. If you believe in luck as a stable force, and you also believe that your personal luck is within your sphere of influence, it follows that you would be more consistent in pursuing your goals. After all, you have an advantage over all those people who aren't as lucky as you.

On the contrary, taking the approach to luck as a random and un-influenceable can make you wonder, "What's the point of even trying?" Being skeptical and simply resigning yourself to your fate will undermine any motivation to make the effort to be successful in the first place.

Let's take an example from the restaurant industry. There are a lot of myths about how many restaurants fail in the first few years after opening, but even conservative estimates put this number somewhere around 60% of restaurants failing within three years. We can imagine that somebody with an external locus of control and a fleeting view on luck might look at that probability for failure and say, "Why even bother? My restaurant would probably fail, anyway."

Retain the same external locus of control, but switch the view on luck from fleeting to stable, and suddenly our prospective restaurant owner might be thinking, "Only 40% succeed, but I'm luckier than most people, so I think I'll be in the 40%."

As the old cliché goes, "You miss 100% of the shots you don't take." Simply believing that you are in some way luckier than average can drastically increase your likelihood of success, because if nothing else, it's going to motivate you to at least try.

It's safe to say only knowing whether somebody believes in luck without knowing whether they view luck as stable or transitory does not give us enough information to properly infer how success-oriented that individual may be. But when we put the two pieces of information together, we can come to a couple of general conclusions.

An external locus of control combined with a stable view on luck will typically result in being "lucky" because these individuals will be looking for more opportunities, similar to their counterparts with internal loci of control.

An external locus of control combined with a fleeting view on luck will typically result in being passive, possibly also leading to a state of learned hopelessness in the absence of feeling in control. If you wanted to lose weight and you felt that nothing you did or ate would make a difference, why would you bother?

Attribution Theory

Austrian psychologist Fritz Heider developed attribution theory, which deals with how we attach meaning to our own behavior and the behavior of other people – for a final look into the psychology of control and luck.

The theory states that people will attach meaning through one of two ways — internal attribution, where a person's success or failure is determined by personality traits; and external attribution, where a person's success or failure is the result of external circumstances. Did the salesman fail to make any sales today because he wasn't charismatic and persuasive enough, or did he simply get unlucky with difficult customers who weren't serious about making a purchase? The story you tell yourself will instantly show you where you lie on the spectrum of attribution.

Sounds similar to the loci of control theory, doesn't it?

Heider believed that we tend to view the failures of others through a lens of *internal attribution*, believing that the person's blunder was caused by internal personality traits. When it is instead ourselves who have erred, we are much more likely to use *external attribution* — blaming the error on situational factors or other people instead of taking personal responsibility for it.

The same theory can be applied in the case of achieving some kind of success. We will be more likely to attribute our own success internally, but the success of others externally, perhaps to "luck." When we succeed, it's because of our intelligence and charm, but when we fail, it's because of our bad luck and external circumstances. It's very convenient and defensive.

Humans are always trying to have their cake and eat it too, being celebrated for success without also being held accountable for failure. It makes sense that our attributions are determined in good part by our emotional and motivational drives. We make self-serving attributions to feel better in our success and to avoid personal ramifications in our failures.

We will also tend toward self-serving attributions in the face of what we view as personal attacks. Instead of addressing the criticism, we will point to other injustices in this unfair world as distractions or excuses. This is especially true for people who have a strong need to avoid failure at all costs, as they will be most likely to make attributions which put themselves in a good light.

But are these self-serving attributions actually harming us long term? If we never take responsibility for our failures, how can we expect to learn from them and not repeat them? Furthermore, if we truly believe that luck is a major factor in our ability to succeed, then we are much less likely to have perseverance and discipline when external circumstances aren't in our favor. This is basically the logic behind making excuses and engaging in rationalizing behaviors.

We also tend to blame victims for their own suffering in a subconscious effort to distance ourselves from suffering the same plight. Yet another tendency we have is to view ourselves as more complicated than others, thinking we are more multifaceted and less predictable because we spend more of our time thinking introspectively than about the complexities of other people.

Ultimately, what can you take away from understanding these natural human tendencies?

If we prefer to think of ourselves as responsible and accountable and generally holding our own fates in our hands, then we do away completely with the concept of luck. This gives you a full path toward victory, but also failure. Perhaps we engage in lucky thinking as a defense mechanism to protect against those inevitable failures. In a way, it can be said that personal responsibility is almost directly in conflict with feelings of luck.

Take two people who have the exact same amount of talent and work equally hard. One goes out for lunch at the very moment the other is discovered by a talent agent eating lunch at his desk. Would this be considered lucky the person was simply hungry for something specific at the right moment? Would this be considered unlucky for the person who stepped out for lunch at the exact wrong moment?

Perhaps.

It might feel like this chapter has been leading up to the point of declaring that a belief in luck is going to hold you back, but that's not quite the point. It's the belief that you can't help your circumstances, and that luck will either make or break you that will hold you back. Realizing that you have the power to change your reality is what will lead to situations we would call lucky.

Luck, to whatever degree you believe in it, will not be the primary factor that determines the outcomes in your life. But it does matter.

Chapter 3. As Seen on Oprah ...

Whatever you think of it, luck is an extremely valuable commodity because of how people seem to clamor for it. And as is the case with any valuable commodity, there are a whole lot of people who want more of it.

We shouldn't be at all surprised, therefore, that there are all kinds of methods out there which supposedly increase people's luck, or otherwise claim to manifest happiness and fulfillment. Whenever there is a need in a market, solutions will spring up, and not all of them are actually targeted at solving the problem. Some of them are just targeted at selling a solution. This chapter will examine two of the most common methods and attempt to determine if they are effective at bringing good fortune, or if they are merely giving people the illusion of having more control over their lives and happiness. As the chapter title notes, these are methods that may have been seen on outlets such as Oprah, or other such shows that tend to hop onto new trends without regard for scientific commentary. In other words, they're buzzwords that might make your raise your eyebrows until you dig into the science.

There may indeed be truly effective ways to be luckier in life, but are these popular notions them?

Visualize and Repeat Affirmations

The first method we're going to put under the microscope is the visualization and affirmation method.

Visualization entails thinking about the goals we want to accomplish or the things we want to attain in our lives and using our imagination to generate an image of those things in our minds. There is no discrimination about what types of good fortune you can visualize having — physical, emotional, mental, and spiritual are all fair game.

You might, for example, visualize yourself being in the best physical shape of your life, parking your Land Rover in the garage of your mansion, being welcomed home by your ideal spouse and adoring children as you walk through the door. Another version of this is to create what's known as a vision board, where you put a picture of everything you want to achieve or attain on a whiteboard so you can see it on a daily basis.

What's key in visualizing is to form as detailed a mental image as possible of what you want to achieve or attain.

The second part of this technique is to repeat positive affirmations about your goals and desires as you maintain the mental image of yourself having achieved and acquired these things in your mind. In other words, you are repeating to yourself about what you want to accomplish and attain. The positive affirmations are repeated frequently — often in front of the mirror — so as to manifest whatever sort of positive energy is required for these visualizations to become reality. For instance, you would look in the mirror and repeat, "I will be rich and own a large house" 10 times each morning.

Sound useless? Well, obviously if you visualize outlandish and impossible things, no amount of positive affirmation will make those things come true. The real question is — in reasonable scenarios — does the visualization and affirmation method actually succeed in creating more desirable outcomes that are associated with luck? These are extremely popular methods to increase self-confidence, feelings of luck, and to extract what you want from life. At first glance, the general idea is to increase your alertness and awareness to your goals. But do these methods you can accomplish from your couch work in reality?

Allen Richardson, an Australian psychologist, attempted to measure the impact of positive mental visualization in a tangible way. He first had all of the study participants shoot free throws (basketball shots), recording data on each player to determine their baseline shooting ability. Richardson then separated the participants into groups:

- Group A - Practiced free throws every day for 20 days
- Group B - Only shot free throws on the first and last days of the study
- Group C - Only shot free throws on the first and last days of the study, but mentally rehearsed shooting the free throws for 20 minutes per day every day in between

On the 20th day, all of the participants were gathered again and asked to shoot free throws.

Group A's shooting percentage increased by an average of 25% with the 20 days of practice. Group B, unsurprisingly, didn't show any improvement from their performances on the first day.

The discovery of the experiment, though, was that Group C's shooting percentage increased by an average of 24%, almost identical to Group A. This occurred despite the fact that Group A had physically practiced shooting free throws for 20 days, while Group C hadn't actually touched a basketball since the first day of the study.

Richardson concluded that positive visualization is indeed a powerful tool to be successful, at least in the case of putting a ball into a hoop. The participants who imagined the ball leaving their hands and traveling on a perfect trajectory until they watched it swish through the net showed truly remarkable improvement in 20 days. It is reasonable to say that they indeed made themselves more effective through positive visualization.

It might even be reasonable to say that one can make themselves luckier through visualizing the outcomes they want. The act of mental rehearsal can make you readier, more open, more aware, and more willing to jump into situations you might not have otherwise. You might find yourself getting better and more opportunities if you visualize them happening. Sounds like luck to me.

Meanwhile, researchers at Carnegie Mellon University attempted to determine if self-affirmations could have a positive impact on performance.

The researchers gathered a group of 73 college students and asked them to rank 11 personal values in order of importance to them. Half of the participants were given an exercise of self-affirmation in which they wrote about what made the values at the tops of their lists so important to them. The other half served as the control group, so they were asked to write about the value they had put ninth on their list.

To measure the effects of the self-affirmations on the participants, they were given a timed problem-solving test and intentionally subjected to stress by an evaluator. The results of the tests showed that the test-takers who had been a part of the self-affirmation group scored better on the test than those from the control group.

These results indicated that self-affirmations can be a beneficial tool people can use to remain calm and think flexibly while under pressure. When we feel stressed and anxious, our brains typically can't operate as smoothly as we'd like. As stress is an undesirable reaction of our mind to stimulation, it's possible that positive self-affirmations can be helpful to anybody who experiences significant pressure to perform in work or school. Affirmations may not expressly help you perform better, but they'll help you *not perform poorly* which is just as important most of the time.

This likely isn't the first time that you've heard about positive visualizations and affirmations, so it's good to know that this method actually does have some scientific merit behind it. The major question remains: Does the visualization and affirmation method legitimately increase your luck?

Kind of, yes.

That's as concrete of an answer as exists. The results of these studies do show that it is possible to positively influence our own mental states. That can definitely be characterized as setting the ground for luck, though not generating luck itself.

More importantly, these studies both illustrate the power of believing in ourselves — not that we are lucky, but that we are capable. These methods — when applied reasonably — are in a way teaching us to shift to a more internal locus of control, where the role of luck is far less significant in our perceptions about the world and our personal abilities. Again, we run into the quandary of personal accountability denying the concept of luck.

The Law of Attraction

If the method of visualization and repeating affirmations is the first step of using positive thinking to create positive outcomes in life, then belief in the Law of Attraction is the logical conclusion of that idea.

The Law of Attraction is the belief that your thoughts by themselves can shape the world around you; that we can color our thoughts with emotion and feeling and those thoughts will then manifest themselves in our lives. You might think about having a life filled with loving relationships and profound happiness, and over time, you will supposedly manifest love and happiness in your life because you desire it and think about it. There are many approaches and definitions to it.

A Google search of the Law of Attraction will yield all kinds of results claiming that it can make a real difference in your life. The *We Shape Life Organization* breaks the method down into seven simple steps:

1. Relax your mind through 5 to 10 minutes of meditation.
2. Think about exactly what you want, creating a clear and detailed image in your mind. Don't allow yourself to have any self-doubt.
3. Ask the universe for what you want.

4. Write your wishes down and feel them happening to you.
5. Feel that your wishes are coming true. Think, speak, and act as if they already have.
6. Show gratitude by recording all of the blessings the universe has bestowed upon you.
7. Be patient and trust the universe.

You can characterize this process however you want, but then again, visualization and positive affirmations don't sound particularly promising to the skeptical mind, either, and we've already learned that there is some merit to that method. The real question is, is there any evidence to also support the Law of Attraction as a legitimate method for improving one's life? Or is it pseudoscience that masquerades as self-help?

In 1999, Lien Pham and Shelley Taylor of the University of California carried out a study to test the efficacy claims of the Law of Attraction. They didn't test the exact tenets of the Law of Attraction, but essentially tested *fantastical thinking*. Fantastical thinking can be thought of as thinking about positive daydreams and fantasies. They broke up the study's participants into three groups:

- Group 1 - Students were asked to spend a few minutes each day visualizing with a clear image how great it would feel to score highly on an important mid-term exam that was coming up in a few days.
- Group 2 - Students were asked to spend a few minutes each day visualizing when, where, and how they intended to study for the exam.
- Group 3 - This was the control group. Students were not asked to visualize anything to do with the exam.

The results were telling. The students from Group 1 studied the least and got the lowest grades on the exam. On the bright side, they did feel better about themselves during the process, but that is a small silver lining considering that their tangible results were contrary to what they had thought about.

Students in Group 2 who visualized themselves studying actually prepared better, studied more, and earned higher marks on the exam than the students from the other groups, while also reporting that they were less stressed about the exam.

Pham and Taylor's study is another point of evidence supporting the benefits of visualization while refuting that the Law of Attraction has an ability to bring us benefit or good fortune. A simple belief in change attracting good luck may not do much good by itself, but visualizing exactly what that change entails does help.

However, one study is certainly insufficient to rule out the Law of Attraction.

A 2015 study published in the *European Journal of Social Psychology* attempted to measure the effects of implementing the Law of Attraction for students to enter romantic relationships with their crushes. A team of four researchers (Oettingen, Kappes, Guttenberg, and Gollwitzer) asked the participants to imagine what would happen in various scenarios where they interacted with their romantic crush in some way.

Their fantasies were rated by the researchers on a spectrum from highly negative to highly positive, with some of the positive fantasies including such clichés as making eye contact across the room and knowing that it was love at first sight. The fantasies that were rated more negatively included some particularly devastating thoughts, with one girl describing her daydreaming thought as, "We are both free and single, he turns to me, smiles and asks how I am. For reasons that I still do not fully understand, I explain that I already have a boyfriend."

Five months later, the researchers reconnected with the study participants to see what had happened with their crushes in that time. On average, those students who had fantasized positively about their crushes had been less likely to be forthcoming about their feelings to the crush, or to otherwise pursue a relationship with them in some way, relative to those who had imagined things working out poorly.

Much like the positive thinkers from the first study, these people may have felt better about themselves by fantasizing, daydreaming, and utilizing the Law of Attraction, but their positive thinking failed to manifest itself tangibly in their actual lives. Wishing for luck brought nothing but complacency.

One of the researchers from the last study, Gabriele Oettingen, conducted another study measuring how positive thinking about career advancement correlated with actual career advancement over a period of two years.

Senior college students were asked to note how often they fantasized about getting their dream job after graduation. When Oettingen followed up with the participants three years later, she learned that the students who had fantasized more frequently about career success had submitted fewer job applications, received fewer job offers, and were working for smaller salaries.

Based on the combined results of these three studies, it seems that the Law of Attraction may in reality be *detrimental*, not helpful, in manifesting what we desire to achieve in our actual lives. Thinking positively makes us feel better, but perhaps feeling better leads to passivity. It's like using a Band-Aid and reducing the pain of a symptom while ignoring the cause of the pain itself. In other words, feeling as if we already have what we desire or that we can attain it through good luck will make us less motivated and less proactive about pursuing our goals and desires. The Law of Attraction is about belief and thought, and even visualization emphasizes process and detail.

So what can we do to take advantage of positive thinking and the power of our minds?

Wishing or fantasizing that we reach our goals and attain all of our desires without action doesn't seem to do anything but harm us, but visualizing taking the actions to make those things happen actually makes us more likely to be proactive. While our positive ideas, thoughts, and dreams can help us determine what we want, by themselves, they don't necessarily lead to action or good luck.

The Law of Attraction is still being pushed because people want to believe that they can achieve everything they desire without putting in the time and effort to actually make it happen, but unfortunately, that remains an unrealistic and perhaps even impossible dream.

The bottom line is, creating "good luck" in our lives is really more about creating the conditions for positive things to happen to us. If you want to work at your dream job and make a higher salary, you'll need to put in the effort to apply for jobs, work hard, and build up your skills and networking connections to realistically qualify yourself for that dream job.

How do you apply the method of visualization and affirmation to reaching goals that are more abstract than shooting free throws better, or not getting stressed out about taking a test? Embrace the process or journey of reaching your goals, rather than focusing on the destination.

Let's say you really want to get into better shape so that you can show off your swimsuit body on your next tropical vacation. Imagining yourself with the body you want won't help you get it, but visualizing yourself working out in the gym or hiking a nearby mountain path just might increase the chances that you actually do those things. Repeating self-affirmations that you are disciplined and hard-working and that you will stick to your exercise regimen — even on the days you feel tired or discouraged — can build your belief in yourself to accomplish your goals. Again, you are creating the conditions for luck, not the positive outcome itself.

If you want to give yourself a mental boost, visualize yourself working through the process of reaching that destination or reward. The real magic is in building up the internal belief that you are capable of creating the conditions for "luck," not that your beliefs can manifest luck into your life in and of themselves. Good luck doesn't come around just by wishing and waiting for it, as much as we may want it to.

Chapter 4. Coincidence and Serendipity

There are two phenomena that humans commonly associate with luck — coincidence and serendipity.

Serendipity is the occurrence and development of favorable or beneficial events, seemingly by chance. It is considered serendipitous, for example, to meet somebody who grew up in the same small town as you while you are both living in an urban metropolis on the other side of the country. Whenever you find yourself saying, "It's a small world," you've probably experienced some serendipity.

Similarly, a coincidence is a remarkable concurrence of events or circumstances with seemingly no casual connection to one another. The word 'coincidence' can be used affirmatively, as in, "It is a crazy coincidence that we wore the same colored shirts as each other three days in a row." However, it is also common to use "coincidence" in the negative, such as, "It can't be a coincidence that we wore the same colored shirts as each other three days in a row." It can also be positive or negative, respectively: "I can't believe we are both from the same village of under 500 inhabitants" or "I can't believe my ex-boyfriend is here out of all the restaurants in this huge city."

While random chance is an inherent part of both phenomena, the more of each we experience personally, the luckier we appear to be. What we really want to know is whether or not these seemingly random events are actually connected somehow, or if they are truly just a result of statistical probabilities. Are there explanations for what we might perceive as luck, coincidence, and serendipity?

Serendipity

We can consider serendipity to be the combination of two main factors — *seemingly improbable occurrences and positive personal feelings about them*. Unexpectedly running into an old friend is serendipitous, especially because it might lead to a profitable professional relationship, a rekindled romance, or even just sharing an enjoyable meal together. On the other hand, when you just as unexpectedly run into an old nemesis and are reminded why you disliked them in the first place — well, that's not serendipitous in the slightest.

Stephen Makri is a prominent lecturer in the field of information interaction at City University London. He's conducted several studies with the intention of better understanding what serendipity is, and the different ways people perceive it in their own lives.

In a study published in 2014, Makri questioned professionals in creative fields about what they do personally to increase their likelihood of experiencing a serendipitous encounter. Most of their answers related to variability in some way or another — mixing things up at the office by working in different environments with different people, or just generally being aware of getting bogged down in an overly repetitive routine so that they can try to change things up more frequently.

Makri summed up his thoughts on the results of his studies and the relationship between luck and serendipity by saying: "I think that luck means different things to different people — some people use it as a synonym for serendipity. But others were clear that the two were different — luck was totally out of our control and there's nothing that we can do to influence it. They think that serendipity can't be controlled but it could be influenced."

One of the interesting things about serendipity or other fortuitous events is that we often don't realize just how beneficial they are until long after the fact. Reminiscing on a lucky event in the past might lead us to an understanding or insight of how it served as a catalyst to create positive change for us. It can sometimes be rewarding, or perhaps even unsettling, to reflect on cause and effect in our own lives, and to realize how small and seemingly innocuous occurrences of the past have had massive impacts on our current selves.

Let's say that you usually eat lunch at your office, but one day you decide to go buy a sandwich from a local deli. As you're waiting in line, you see an old friend from high school, Mary. You and Mary make the usual small-talk while catching up, and when you tell Mary you're working as a graphic designer, she says that she has another friend in the business she could connect you with. You say that you would appreciate that, exchange information, and go your separate ways.

In a vacuum, the significance of this interaction is rather ambiguous, and calling it serendipitous would seem premature unless catching up with Mary was the most exciting thing to happen all day.

Now imagine that you and Mary weren't that close, and re-establishing a relationship with her isn't really worth the effort to you. You never follow up with her, and this is the end of the tale.

But what if instead, you've been struggling to add new clients online and you simply can't pass up the networking opportunity, so you follow up with Mary and get in touch with her friend. Mary's recommendation starts you off on the right foot, and from there, you develop a business partnership and friendship with her friend that lasts for years.

If you hadn't chosen to eat at the deli instead of in your office like usual, you might never have run into Mary, connected with her friend, and benefited both professionally and personally for years as a result. Suddenly, this is one of the most serendipitous events of your life.

The real difference between status quo and serendipity, however, was in the effort you put in afterward. Being open, positive, and proactive makes people more likely to recognize and appreciate an opportunity so that they will take advantage of the potential good fortunate they receive.

In reality, serendipitous events are simply good things that have a low probability of occurring. As such, we can increase our chances of serendipity just by putting ourselves in situations where — however improbable — good things can happen to us. You're not going to have a moment of serendipity at home watching television, but just walking outside raises the probability one notch higher. Going to a social event with somebody you don't hang out with often will bump it up again. Doing new things with different people constantly will all but guarantee a steady flow of opportunities that could be seen as serendipitous in hindsight.

Of course, the opposite is true as well. Bad luck is far more likely to fall upon you when you are constantly doing new things with different people than if you stayed at home safe and sound. So it's a reasonable conclusion that our perceptions about reality, and luck specifically, are important factors in how lucky or unlucky we end up being.

Coincidence

When you want to encompass the full spectrum of improbable occurrences that happen in our lives — from serendipitous to terribly misfortunate — you call them coincidences. All serendipity is a coincidence by virtue of it occurring despite having a low probability that it would, but not all coincidences are serendipitous, unfortunately.

There are two sides to the "I don't believe in coincidences" coin, however. On one side, there are the people who believe that all coincidences are really just signs with a deeper meaning — whether it's coming from the universe or some other force — pointing them toward some sort of personal enlightenment or enrichment. On the other side of the coin are those who say that believing in coincidences is a result of a lack of understanding about statistical probabilities.

In 1989, mathematicians Persi Diaconis and Frederick Mosteller published a paper titled *Methods for Studying Coincidences*. At first, they considered a broad definition of the term as encompassing all rare events, but eventually settled on the definition: "A coincidence is a surprising concurrence of events, perceived as meaningfully related, with no apparent casual connection."

Interestingly, coincidences shouldn't really be that surprising from a statistical point of view, because they happen all the time. As statistician David Hand put it in his book, *The Improbability Principle,* "Extremely improbable events are commonplace."

What makes them seem crazy, strange, or extraordinary then? What makes us lose our minds over them and proclaim great or terrible luck? Mostly, we stink at calculating probabilities.

Our brains are in some ways just like computers — processing information as efficiently as they can and conserving as much energy as possible. But given our processing rate and all of the complexities of cause and effect, it is inefficient or even impossible for us to objectively calculate probabilities as we go about our daily lives. We can estimate, but our accuracy is not likely to be particularly noteworthy.

Add in the fact that there are now over 7.5 billion people in the world, and the opportunities for statistical improbabilities to occur are everywhere. Diaconis and Mosteller's *Law of Truly Large Numbers* states, "With a large enough sample, any outrageous thing is likely to happen." The odds that your one lottery ticket will win the Powerball are infinitesimally small, but the odds that somebody's —anybody's — ticket will win it are actually considerable. The winner will feel they have been blessed with incredibly good fortune, but the buyers of the millions of tickets that win nothing likely won't think twice about it — after all, they didn't have a high probability to win in the first place.

This also harkens back to the classic example of probability — if you were to put an infinite number of monkeys into a room with typewriters and wait for an infinite amount of time, it is a statistical eventuality that one of them would bang out a perfect recreation of Shakespeare's *Romeo and Juliet*.

When you begin to look at coincidences as low probabilities, it actually begins to seem inevitable that you'll experience some from time to time. When you think about all of the people you personally know and all the places you go, and then consider all of the places that all of the people you know are going — chances are good that you'll bump into somebody you know, somewhere, at some point. For instance, if you live in the same city as someone, are near the same age, have overlapping friends and interests, and have similar diets, there really aren't so many places you would both spend time.

The 49 times that we go to the grocery store, shop, and check out without seeing any friends or acquaintances don't register, but that one time that you see an old teacher from a class you were in over a decade ago is probably going to give your brain a big jolt of nostalgia, thus highlighting the coincidence.

And those are just the coincidences that are actually realized. How many near-coincidences have you learned about after the fact? You might be talking to a friend and find out that you randomly ate lunch at the same restaurant on the same day, but sat on opposite sides of the restaurant and just didn't see each other. When you start to include the close calls, the probability of some coincidence occurring at some point suddenly seems even greater.

The further we examine these ideas, the more apparent it becomes that luck might just be an inaccurate way of describing these external events and circumstances. We may not have enough information to do the math behind the cause and effect that creates our present reality, but we can still accept that it is there.

Psychiatrist and author of the book *Connecting with Coincidence,* Bernard Beitman, studied how various personality traits relate to views on coincidences. He found that people who describe themselves as religious, spiritual, or otherwise seeking a higher meaning in life have greater likelihoods of seeing coincidences in their lives. Likewise, self-referential (likely to relate external information back to themselves) people are also prone to experience more coincidences. Coincidence, like luck, is a tool that humans use to make ourselves feel better when we feel sad, angry, or anxious by creating meaning from all the natural chaos around us.

According to Beitman, there are three categories of coincidences — environment-environment interactions, mind-environment interactions, and mind-mind interactions.

Environment-environment interactions are those coincidences which are objectively observable in the physical world. Your run into your high school sweetheart in a foreign city after not seeing each other in 10 years, and it leads to a rekindled romance. These are the most obvious and easiest to understand of the coincidences.

Slightly less objective are the mind-environment interactions, which are ones where you randomly think about something or somebody and then some event relating to that thing or person happens in your life. This might be thinking about a friend you haven't caught up with in months and then receiving a text from that friend later the same day. These premonition-esque coincidences might feel cool, but they are also highly difficult to measure.

The last category, mind-mind interactions, are uncommon and might even seem mystical. Beitman coined the term "simulpathity" to describe a mind-mind interaction in which one person actually experiences the pain or emotion of somebody else who is far away. This is most frequently reported between twins, and while it is the least associable form of coincidence with luck, it is certainly an interesting phenomenon to ponder.

It can be difficult to change your perception about coincidences. Maybe you don't even want to because believing in them seems like a harmless thing people do to make ourselves feel better. But in reality, understanding coincidences for what they are doesn't necessarily change the feelings those coincidences elicit in us. You can understand that running into an old friend in an unexpected place is statistically probable to happen every once in a while, yet still be grateful and excited when it does happen.

Furthermore, thinking in terms of probabilities allows you to manipulate those probabilities in your favor, if you so choose, by constantly doing new things with new people in different places so you have more opportunities to experience low-probability occurrences. Clearly, this correlates with greater luck.

With that in mind, let's examine something referred to as the birthday paradox to better grasp the math behind our coincidences. Given a sample size of 23 people, there is a 50-50 chance that two people will have the same birthday. At first, this is counterintuitive. There are 365 days in a year, so how could such a small sample size create even odds? The reason this doesn't immediately compute is that our brains struggle to do computation with exponents.

With 23 people, there are 253 chances for a matching birthday. The first person has 22 people to compare with, the next has 21, and so on. Summing all of the numbers from 22 down to 1 gives us 253. Now the chance that any 2 people have *different* birthdays is 364/365 — this is the number in the back of your head making the 50-50 odds so confusing. However, when we take the fraction 364/365 and raise it to the exponent 253, we get the result 0.4995, or approximately 50%.

Essentially, each of the 253 times that there is a chance for two people to have the same birthday, we are multiplying the fraction 364/365 by itself, reducing it ever so slightly and increasing the odds of two people out of the 23 having the same birthday.

We simply can't do this calculation in our heads, much like the probabilities of the vast majority of the coincidental and serendipitous occurrences of our lives. But whether we can do the calculations or not, the math is still there, governing the seemingly random occurrences of our lives. And of course, it's easy to interpret much of this as fortuitous luck.

Chapter 5. Traits for Luck

It might seem like luck is something you are born to be. Fortunately, being lucky has nothing to do with birth, innate ability, or even talent. If there's been a theme throughout this book thus far, it is that luck is achievable through creating conditions for luck — and that is wholly within your control.

Truly being lucky boils down to a short aphorism by the Roman philosopher and statesman, Seneca: "Luck is where opportunity meets preparation."

In Ancient Rome, Seneca lived a life that defined luck. He was born into a low rank, but through his hard work and awareness, he moved up into the realm of the elite in Rome. His "luck" brought him a friendship with Roman emperors, including Claudius and Nero. He eventually became one of the wealthiest people of his day.

Was Seneca luckier than most people? He certainly wasn't unlucky. But he also understood the workings of the world which is clear throughout the philosophical texts he crafted in his lifetime. He embodied several of the traits that modern researchers and psychologists consider to be those of lucky people.

Lucky Traits

There are a handful of traits which are common in people who consider themselves to be lucky.

Richard Wiseman, a psychologist who has extensively studied luck, has found that people who are lucky find themselves in a certain state of mind that makes them more aware of lucky occurrences. You can call it a lucky mindset, or simply the tendency to get themselves into situations many people would call lucky. In several experiments relating to luck, he found that those who achieve it have tend to have three consistent personality traits.

Those three personality traits for luck include variations on the spectrums of extroversion, openness, and neuroticism. Wiseman found that people with those three traits were available to opportunities that turned into lucky moments. These three traits seemed to give people a better chance at being in the right place at the right time and maximizing their opportunities for great outcomes.

Extroversion

Extroversion is the first trait Wiseman found to be highly correlated with luck.

According to the *Big 5 Factors theory* of personality, extroversion is defined by people being assertive, energetic, and talkative.

Someone who shows extroversion is likely to be lucky due to an enthusiastic involvement with the outside world. Extroverts have an easy time talking to anyone, so they often have opportunities to meet interesting people.

Extroverts become highly energized when they are around other people. They are likely to become the life of any party. They are easy to notice in crowds because of their talkative and energetic personalities, which could explain why lucky things happen to them. If we take luck to be a quantity which increases with exposure and experience, extroverts are necessarily luckier because they crave that exposure. The more opportunities you come across, even bad ones, you will find an equal proportion of good ones. The more you try, the more you discover and experience. Simply, you're going to have more lucky breaks when you meet ten people a day versus none.

Openness

When someone demonstrates a high level of openness, they are relaxed about life and ready to experience new circumstances. They are not as risk-averse as others and don't make decisions through a perspective of fear and anxiety. When opportunity knocks on the door of someone with an open mind, that person will answer the door and investigate the challenge. They'll not only open the door, they'll walk down that path and consider if they even want to return the way they came. Someone with a closed mind will not do any of these things.

It is relatively easy to identify someone who has a high level of openness; this is the person who doesn't say no to anything, whether you suggest it or they do. Let's say you want to go skydiving, but you want to go with a friend. The friend who is open to new ideas is the one you will call.

People who are open tend to land in the luckiest circumstances. They end up with the best jobs because they make themselves aware of opportunities. They also seem to be the people who end up backstage at concerts, with the autographs at ballparks, and as winners in contests. These things happen to them because they are open to the opportunities and they jump on them. They may not readily identify everything as a positive opportunity, but just as importantly, they don't rule anything out.

Neuroticism

Finally, neuroticism is technically a state of being *neurotic*, which often includes anxiety, nervousness, and jealousy. Essentially, this is the trait of being high-strung and perpetually on guard. Unlike the other two traits, Wiseman found that those at the opposite end, with low levels of neuroticism, were likely to have more luck in their lives that those at the high-level end.

Why is this?

Someone who shows low levels of neuroticism will be calmer and more relaxed than someone who is at the high end of the spectrum. When people are calm and focused, they become highly aware of their surroundings without being anxious. Someone in a relaxed state of mind allows themselves to be open to opportunity and even happiness, where someone who is perpetually anxious will be endlessly preoccupied by perceived slights, insults, and alarms.

Someone with low neuroticism also sees what is happening around them, and is therefore often lucky. For example, while many people walk down the street listening to music or focused on their phones, the low neuroticism person will often walk down the street taking in the ambiance and the view. They don't feel threatened by letting their guards down. This is why people with low neuroticism become so lucky — because they are paying attention to the world and choosing not to become closed off to it. When their minds are not preoccupied with anxiety, they are able to be present and explore what's in front of them.

How Wiseman Tested Luck

One of Wiseman's studies clearly showed how openness and awareness can play a major factor in what we consider "luck." In his experiment, he asked volunteers to count the number of photographs in a newspaper. On page two of the newspaper, there was a headline that read "STOP COUNTING—THERE ARE 43 PHOTOGRAPHS IN THIS NEWSPAPER." Further down the page was another headline that read "STOP COUNTING, TELL THE EXPERIMENTER YOU HAVE SEEN THIS AND WIN $250."

Everyone in the study missed the headlines, but they did count all 43 photographs. Wiseman concluded that people were too focused (too neurotic) on the goal. They failed to relax and see the opportunities that were right in front of their faces.

Even though these three personality traits contribute to lucky events, the real reason people tend to be lucky is that they are involved in the world around them. Like Seneca said, it takes work. But Wiseman found that along with work, relaxation helps too. People who try too hard to find opportunities miss them more often than not because they end up making themselves blind to anything else. So, when it comes luck — balance between being relaxed and alert helps. This is the balance between being open, calm, and extroverted.

Recall that luck is mostly random and is somewhat self-generated. No one can predict what will happen to them, but they can manage their reactions to those events. By being calm and relaxed, open to opportunities, and involved in life, it is easier to jump on those random events and become "lucky."

In addition to the those traits, optimism is a driver of good fortune. Optimists look at the bright side of life, seeking and anticipating that good things will happen. Lucky people tend to be optimists because they act like they are going to succeed. For instance, you will prepare for a long car ride far differently than you would prepare for a 10-minute ride. The way you view something drastically changes your actions.

Along with adding optimism to your daily routine, it is helpful to develop a sense of humility. If you are not afraid of being embarrassed in unexpected situations, then you will be open and free to try new things. By being calm and accepting that you might fail, you will be surprised by the good things that come your way. If you are instead defensiveness and afraid of judgment and rejection, you will probably close yourself off from most chances for luck because the cost (embarrassment) simply won't be worth the benefit (an opportunity). A little bit of vulnerability can make you far luckier if you are just willing to take a leap of faith more frequently.

Take, for example, the professional baseball player. Every time a professional baseball player goes up to bat, he has a roughly 72% chance of failing in front of hundreds of thousands of people on TV and in the stadium. But he expects it and is okay with the potential for failure. If the baseball player did not take that chance of failure, he could never become the hero who hits the big home run to win the game. At the plate, the batter has to be calm, optimistic, vulnerable, and completely ready to accept failure. This also underlies openness.

Finally, you can change your luck by being proactive. Being lucky involves more than just showing up; you actually have to get engaged in life. You have to search for opportunities, because they will not land in your lap if you are not out there seeking them.

Along with Seneca and Machiavelli's words of wisdom, the Latin aphorism "Carpe Diem" is another excellent way to live a lucky life. This aphorism is a proclamation to live life to the fullest without fear of the future. Instead of shying away for fear of looking silly or the possibility of failing, lucky people try new things and give it their best shot.

When you get involved with life, sometimes you win and sometimes you lose. But do you skip taking a vacation because you are afraid of the small chance the plane could crash with you on it? If you don't get on the plane, then you do not get to see the world. If you do not buy the lottery card, then you cannot win the $1 million prize. If we let fear keep us back, then we miss out on all of the wonderful things that could happen. The old "shoulda-coulda-woulda" syndrome.

Luck doesn't come to those people who said, "I wish I would have taken that job," or "I should have gone on that date," or "If only I could have another chance, I would do it differently."

No, luck comes to people who take the job, go on the date, and do it the first time. Luck presents itself in random ways, and it is up to you to recognize it and accept the opportunity. The universe speaks in mysterious ways and we cannot open our eyes to it if we are always worried about the plane crashing.

Richard Wiseman saw it several times. In his psychological studies to understand why some people are luckier than others, he has presented strangers with opportunities that many would consider lucky. In many situations, he has literally placed luck right in front of them. Some completely miss it. But others immediately spot the opportunity.

Wiseman's three personality traits for lucky can be more accurately said to create situations for luck to thrive. You too can embody them in small ways. Seneca was on to something when he realized that recognizing opportunities is the key to finding luck. It happens when you seize the moment and don't let fear get in the way. Relax, stay calm, look around, and take the chance when the chance arrives.

Chapter 6. The Four Factors

"You gotta ask yourself one question. 'Do I feel lucky?' Well, do ya, punk?"

Clint Eastwood's *Dirty Harry* famously asked this pivotal question in 1971, but it's a question as old and mysterious as time itself. Do I feel lucky? What makes me lucky? And what is luck, anyway? Again, we end up at the laurels of British professor Richard Wiseman's studies and conclusions on the role kismet plays in our lives.

Over the course of ten years, Wiseman interviewed hundreds of people about the ways luck factored into their daily lives, and numerous patterns emerged. Eventually Wiseman detailed his conclusions in the book *The Luck Factor*, in which he reveals that while his subjects had almost no insights into the causes of their luck, they displayed consistent patterns of behavior that were directly responsible for their good or bad fortune.

We've covered some of these results earlier in the book, and this chapter builds on the narrative of certain traits and factors that typically accompany the presence of luck.

Wiseman conducted many controlled experiments that allowed him to observe "luck" in action. In one experiment, he simply asked volunteers to walk up the street to a specific coffee shop and order a cup of coffee. Unbeknownst to his subjects, he had left money on the ground in their path and had positioned a well-connected businessman inside the shop. A young man who described himself as lucky discovered the money and pocketed it on his way to the shop, and randomly struck up a conversation with the businessman while waiting for his beverage.

A different volunteer, who self-described as unlucky, stepped right over the cash and kept to herself while at the coffee shop.

The vastly different experiences of the volunteers demonstrates Wiseman's notion that some personality types are luckier because they create scenarios which maximize opportunities, and thereby increase their luck. Each volunteer was presented with identical opportunities, but their individual mindsets dictated their course of action. Had the unlucky woman widened her focus just a bit, she would have picked up the money and enjoyed a free cup of coffee. But with her unlucky mindset, she didn't expect the unusual bonus, didn't look for it, and missed it completely. Likewise, her unwillingness to chat up a stranger while waiting for coffee could have cost her a valuable connection.

The primary difference between these two volunteers, says Wiseman, is that the "lucky" man was open to chance opportunities, thereby making him likelier to notice the unexpected in his environment.

This openness, similar to the trait described in a previous chapter, is the first of four factors which determine luck.

Be Open to New Experiences

Lucky people are open to new possibilities. They tend to be somewhat relaxed about life, adopting the general attitude that everything is all right. Wiseman found that they have lower levels of anxiety than their unlucky counterparts, which frees them to not only expect good things, but to actively look for them. According to the professor, unlucky people are frequently stuck in routines. These routines focus on the end goals versus the process or journey. They have a tendency to hyper-focus on accomplishing specific tasks, and as a result, they are blinded to other possibilities. The old saying, "If you do what you've always done, you'll get what you always get" is applicable here. Remaining within your comfort zone assures that new experiences are unlikely to come your way, and if they do, you are apt to miss them.

The takeaway here is to relax your focus and be open to unexpected possibilities. Anything can turn into something, if you allow it to.

Listen to Your Gut

The second factor affecting luck is to listen to your intuition. Lucky people are more willing to take a risk by following their gut instinct. The willingness to take action may be the key. Unlucky people are usually reticent to act until they can prove the move is sound. They frequently suffer from "analysis paralysis." Born of anxiety, analysis paralysis is the inability to act swiftly or decisively and to overthink ideas or situations. Frequently, by the time a situation has been thoroughly examined, the opportunity to act upon it has passed.

Wiseman suspects that our brains are wired in such a way that intuition represents a pattern that is detected by our body and brain, but that our conscious mind has not yet recognized. Our lifetime of experiences and interactions are stored in the pathways of the brain, and it identifies and responds to familiar stimuli much faster than we can perceive. Trusting a hunch frequently yields a greater benefit than creating an exhaustive list of pros and cons. Lucky people realize that if they have a strong gut feeling, it is often worth their time to stop and consider it. This is all to say that our gut hunches and intuition are far smarter than we realize, and by listening to them, we put ourselves in situations that turn out to be fortuitous and lucky.

Case in point: Apple co-founder Steve Jobs takes a calligraphy class.

On a whim, college dropout Jobs decided to take a calligraphy class, where he learned about serif and sans-serif fonts, varying the amount of space between letter combinations, and what makes beautiful typography an art form. The class had no practical application in his life until ten years later when he was designing the first Macintosh computer. The Mac incorporated multiple typefaces and proportionally spaced fonts, revolutionary concepts that have since become industry standards. Said Jobs, "Of course it was impossible to connect the dots looking forward when I was in college. But it was very, very clear looking backwards ten years later. So you have to trust that the dots will somehow connect in your future. You have to trust in something — your gut, destiny, life, karma, whatever. This approach has never let me down, and it has made all the difference in my life."

He followed his instinct to learn about the elements of what makes a beautiful product, which eventually became Apple's hallmark and claim to business immortality – beautiful design and functionality. There may not have been an immediate payoff for Jobs' relative gamble, but it showed that his inkling that elements of calligraphy would be central to his career was correct.

Positive Expectations

Lucky people are certain that their futures are full of good fortune.

They tend to be optimistic and to hope for the best. That optimism gives lucky people more "grit," says Wiseman. In other words, when people hold the belief that things will work out, they are apt to persevere. Perseverance in turn builds resilience, which allows a person to hold fast, giving more time for events to work out in their favor. Optimistic people look on the bright side, and as a result, they have less anxiety and tend to discover unrealized opportunities in misfortune. They understand that they are capable of handling what life throws at them, and this allows them to have a more relaxed attitude because suddenly not every little thing is a life-or-death matter.

They are also more willing to reach out for help and support during times of crisis, which not only lowers their anxiety level, but provides others with new opportunities to utilize their own life experiences and expertise. Given the opening, people love to help, and these types of positive interactions benefit all the involved parties, once again increasing the luck factor.

That doesn't mean that lucky people don't experience setbacks — it just means that their attitude toward the outcome differs greatly from that of the unlucky. The experiences of Chuck Noland in the movie *Castaway* come to mind. As a successful Federal Express systems engineer, Chuck travels the world resolving productivity issues at FedEx terminals until his plane crashes in the Pacific Ocean. As the only survivor, Chuck is forced to adapt to life on a remote island for four years until he is rescued.

Throughout the film, Chuck exhibits positive expectations despite his grim circumstances. He continually hopes for the best while demonstrating resilience in preparing for the worst. He learns how to spearfish for food and creates conveniences for himself from the FedEx cargo that washes up on the beach. He even fashions a buddy, Wilson, out of a volleyball, thus creating "human" interaction for himself and keeping a lively discussion of ideas and plans alive in the face of a bleak future.

Here, it is elements of hope, optimism, and the choice to be happy that contribute to luck. It's no wonder many philosophers have named hope as the most important trait a person can possess.

<u>Transform Bad Luck into Good</u>

One specific technique employed by the character of Chuck Noland is "counterfactual thinking." According to psychologists, the degree to which you think that something is fortunate (or not) is the degree to which you imagine alternatives that are better (or worse).

In other words, lucky people always look for the silver lining. In Noland's case, he reasoned that he could have died in the plane crash, or been eaten by sharks. In his mind, he was lucky to have survived, even if that meant living alone on an island. Therefore, one of the key characteristics for transforming bad luck into good is the ability to face adversity and take control of the situation, not be buried by it. Trust that life has prepared you to handle whatever comes along. Or if a situation is outside your experience, know that others can help and be willing to accept their support. Actively look for the unseen opportunity in misfortune.

Professor Wiseman gives this example: Unlucky people say, "I can't believe I've been in another car accident." Lucky people say, "Yes, I had a car accident, but I wasn't killed." The point is that both ways of thinking are unconscious and automatic. It would never occur to the unlucky people to see it a different way. This gives them the ability to keep on moving and adapt.

Make Your Own Luck

Examining Wiseman's four factors of luck, it is clear that mindset is the key factor.

The way you perceive the events of your life determines whether or not you feel lucky. Optimism, perseverance, and resilience are significant characteristics that differentiate good luck from bad. A relaxed, open attitude toward life is another contributing factor. Professor Wiseman notes, "Lucky people create, notice, and act upon the chance opportunities in their lives."

Create — notice — act. These qualities are the hallmarks of people with good luck. *Create* scenarios where you are interacting with and meeting new people. If activities like networking don't come naturally, attach yourself to someone who knows how to work a room, and ask them to include you. When someone mentions a topic that interests you, maximize the opportunity to talk with them about it. *Notice* the myriad opportunities that continually surround you. If you are frantic or stressed or goal-driven, learn how to slow down and relax so you don't miss the available prospects.

Make space in your busy brain for new experiences. *Act* quickly when your instinct sends you a strong signal. Pay attention, but not too hard. Don't overthink it — trust that your unconscious has detected a pattern and is urging you to make an effective, beneficial decision.

Professor Wiseman makes one final distinction — there is a difference between chance and luck. He reminds us that chance events are like winning the lottery. They are events over which we have no control, other than buying a ticket. When people say that they consistently experience good fortune, he believes, it has to be because of something they are doing. We have far more control over events than we perceive. You might believe that 50% of life is due to chance events. It is not — perhaps 10% is attributed solely to chance. That other 40% you think you're having no influence over at all is actually defined by the way you think, embodied in these four factors and traits.

Chapter 7. "Strategic Luck Planning"

Again, we are faced with the question: Is there actually a way to control and increase your luck? Is there a *strategy* to boost your chances of success?

We know Richard Wiseman's stance — absolutely there is, and they are encapsulated in eight (well, seven and a half) factors and personality traits one can cultivate. However, according to Max Gunther, there are actually 13 types of mindsets to have, rather than characteristics. Gunther was an author and researcher who was best known for his controversial bestseller on financial risk management, *The Zurich Axioms,* but he also wrote other works including *The Luck Factor; The Very, Very Rich;* and *Instant Millionaires.*

His book on *strategic luck planning* outlines 13 different techniques for discovering and taking advantage of life's good breaks. Some people are born with good fortune, while others need a little more strategy to get what they desire. Either way, these 13 steps will ensure your path to success through luck.

Luck vs. Planning

The first of Gunther's rules is that luck and planning are two separate things that should never be confused. When a desired outcome is brought about by luck, you must acknowledge that fact. However, if you take the time to plan for the unexpected and things end up going well, luck is not involved.

If you end up confusing luck with planning, you all but guarantee that your luck will turn bad in the long run. Planning for something and then thinking it was just luck would take away the importance of all the planning that you have put in, and in the future, you may not repeat what caused your success.

We live in a complex and unpredictable world. The first step for improving your luck is to recognize that it exists, but that you aren't successful just because of it. Be humble when you win, and don't be hard on yourself when you lose. After all, without the occasional loss, there would be no reason to improve. Learn from your mistakes, observe what happened, what could have been done better, and how external factors affected the outcome. If planning was why you were successful, then do it again. If it was luck, then find a way to ensure planning would have the same effect.

Find the Fast Flow

Have you ever thought to yourself that nothing ever happens to you? That events and opportunities just pass you by? This may be because you don't position yourself in the best situations. Even if you are a quiet person, all you need to do is go to where the events flow fastest. Surround yourself with a churning mass of people and things will inevitably happen. All you need is to meet a lot of people and let them know who you are. The rest will come naturally and they will direct opportunities your way.

There is no use sitting around waiting for things to just fall in your lap. Go where things are happening. Be curious, put your best foot forward, be interested in people, and make conversation. When you meet someone, ask about their life, their goals, their passions. Some of the most interesting people you will ever meet could be right in front of you, if only you had the initiative to look. The more activity churning around you, the more luck will be included. This doesn't happen if you confine yourself to your room each night.

Take Calculated Risks

There are two ways to guarantee unsuccessfulness.

One is to take risks that are out of proportion to the rewards being sought. For example, putting all your money toward an investment that you haven't properly researched is a recipe for disaster, because even though the reward might be large, the chances of failure outweigh this reward.

The other way to ensure a lack of success and a lack of luck is to not take any risks at all, even when a perfect opportunity presents itself, like not wanting to talk to someone attractive even though you have been assured by three separate people that they like you. Think of it as extreme risk-aversion.

Lucky people avoid both extremes.

Good luck is all about getting a favorable outcome from an uncertain situation. The best way to do this is to take calculated risks that are supported by the evidence and data, anticipating the possible disasters and knowing how to deal with them.

To truly succeed, you need to understand the difference between foolish and calculated risks and know that some risk-taking is infinitely better than none at all. You can't sit on the sidelines and expect to be successful, but you can't leap at every opportunity that is shiny. You must walk a thin line which can only be ascertained through experience, practice, and failure.

<u>Cut Your Losses</u>

This point is all about something that affects us all: greed.

Say you're on a lucky streak and things just keep going your way. We have the tendency to believe that this will continue, but unfortunately, this will never be the case. You can call this arrogance, the Gambler's Fallacy, or a simple lack of foresight. Knowing when to cut your losses and walk away is an important part of the road to success. You need to always assume that a run of luck is going to be short and never try to ride a run to its peak. With this kind of thinking, the law of averages is heavily on your side, and you will be more likely to succeed if you accept that based on probability, your luck will eventually run out.

Don't delude yourself into thinking that something good will last forever, or that you have it all figured out. You will end up losing everything before you know it. It may be hard to accept that there was a chance that you would have won something more, but it will always be harder to accept that you ended up losing it all. You might be lucky, but you won't be lucky forever, so don't depend on it.

Select Your Luck

This is a carryover from the last point. It is important to realize that some opportunities will never lead to great things. All investments, whether they be time, money, or love, will encounter problems. What you need to ask yourself is whether there is a likelihood that they will go away. Do you have some realistic hope of fixing them? If so, then stay aboard. If not, then you should get out and look for better luck elsewhere. In a sense, selecting your luck means knowing where good luck will flow.

Sometimes we can be so sure of an idea, whether it's a career, relationship, business investment, or something else. Perhaps you landed a job that seemed thrilling to you and eventually you realized there was no hope of progression in that position. Sometimes what seemed like a great idea in the beginning doesn't always work out when implemented. Never fall in love with an idea, there might be something better that comes along soon. People can struggle to change their paths because it means that they were wrong. That's okay! What's worse is to stay on a sinking ship with no hope of survival.

Take the Zig-Zag Path

Despite what many people think, the path to success is rarely a straight line.

Even the most well-thought-out plan doesn't always work, and keeping to the same path may lead you nowhere. Lucky people do not have trouble deviating from their course. It's not that they intend to deviate, but they are simply open to the deviation and seize opportunity when it comes because it might be a better path overall.

Plans work best when they are used as a guide, and if something better comes along, the plan should be discarded immediately and without regret. It's not uncommon to have a set goal in mind, perhaps a career that you have always dreamt of, and begin to realize the job you have might not be the best to get you there.

Change can be difficult but sometimes it can lead to the best outcome. Try a different job, accept opportunities with arms wide open, exploit a newly discovered talent, take advantage of serendipity, and if these things don't work out, then find something else. It's impossible to predict what will happen in the future, so don't take long-term plans seriously. They can act as a guide, but unforeseen opportunities are the ones that will really get you places. Nobody has ever had an easy path to success, and you should always be prepared and willing to veer off your chosen course. The zig-zag path, in hindsight, looks incredibly lucky and fortuitous when in reality, you were just okay with discarding plans and taking risks.

Supernatural Belief

Gunther refers to supernaturalism as any belief in an unseen spirit, force, or agency whose existence has not been proved to anyone's satisfaction. But how can this belief help you? It's not because it makes you luckier, but because it helps you make impossible choices. Sometimes there is no rational choice to make, but the worse reaction is to do nothing.

A supernatural belief can help people get into a potentially winning position by helping them make choices. For example, lucky numbers and omens may not be proven, but it can help you take a quick leap of faith into a decision that you may not have been able to make otherwise.

Use superstition and be irrational when things are in your favor, and be rational when they aren't. Who cares if the planets truly did align or if it was just in your mind, as long as it gives you the confidence to take action? This is related to taking a zig-zag path in that deviating from what is planned or conventional, or even realistic, is sometimes the best course of action for luck.

Be A Bit Pessimistic

Lucky people, as a breed, tend to be pessimistic. Optimism means expecting the best, but good luck involves knowing how you'll handle the worst. As discussed earlier, good luck often means taking risks, but it doesn't mean being foolish about it. In order to avoid bad luck, you need to know how to handle the worst-case scenario. Therefore, they don't necessarily see a glass as half-empty, but they do think about how to handle it if it were indeed half-empty. In essence, lucky people hope for the best but are prepared for the worst.

Think about what is the worst that could happen in any situation, and then come up with a solution to protect yourself from these outcomes.

Written agreements, budget plans, or getting insurance are examples of how you have protect yourself from the worst. Lucky people plan ahead and are accountable. They cross their t's and dot their i's to set themselves up for luck and success as best they can. But make sure you don't let your pessimism keep you from trying, or cause you to give up. Use your pessimism to your advantage, but don't let it hold you back.

Shut Up

When given the opportunity, we can often talk ourselves into a variety of situations that are not what we want. Talk can tie you up and lock you into positions that may seem right today but may be wrong tomorrow. When there is no good reason to say something, say nothing. Any opinion has the ability to polarize people, and you never know who you are going to polarize.

Lucky people are careful of what they say and to whom they say it. They don't take strong positions in controversial topics if they can avoid it. Talk has a way of spreading like wildfire, especially if it wasn't the intention. Too much talk can constrict your choices, and you may find yourself in a situation where you think, "Why did I agree to this?" Remember that finding new plans and taking random opportunities are the keys to success, and you can't do this if you've talked yourself into something that you can't get out of. Mind your tongue, because it can pigeon-hole you or even burn bridges before you know it. On the other hand, being a neutral presence as a default can work in your favor.

Recognize a Non-Lesson

A non-lesson is an experience in life which seems to be a lesson, but actually isn't. Not everything means something or implies something. You need to recognize when something was just bad luck and move on. In fact, it may not have even been bad luck — it was just a random event that you can't make any conclusions from. You can't learn anything about how to get better luck here, either.

Do not generalize or create theories out of random events or it will just lead to you avoid things you have no reason to avoid. If you have several bad dating experiences, it doesn't mean all men or women are impossible to date. It only means you have had a few bad experiences and you need to improve how you choose people.

By following non-lessons, you risk missing out on many good things in life just because of bad luck or a few bad experiences. Be wary of these fallacies and don't let them guide your decisions. This is tough because we are powerfully conditioned to seek pleasure and avoid pain, so it requires getting past that instinct and removing the fear from anything negative you've experienced.

Accept that the Universe is Unfair

All of us, even the most optimistic, have had the occasional thought that the universe is out to get us. Although this may be counterproductive in some cases, it is important to accept that life is hard, and most times, unfair. All of us — the good, the bad, and the in-between — are equally as likely to achieve our greatest dreams or live through our worst nightmares. You might be unlucky a few times in a row, and there will be nothing to make up for that fact.

Kids get terminal diseases, people who don't try can end up succeeding, good people will be unlucky, and bad people will have good luck.

Happy endings are just not the norm in life, and you should never expect good things to happen because you deserve it. You don't deserve good luck, and you shouldn't expect a break. We will all experience bad luck regardless of our hard work or good intentions because of how little is actually in our control. The important thing is to accept that everyone has it hard and probably thinks the universe is against them, as well. Accepting that things will always be unfair will prevent you from anger, self-torture, or giving up.

Be Willing To Be Busy

Have you ever noticed that people with the most opportunities are those who seem to be the busiest? This is because the more activities you have going on, the greater the likelihood that an opening could present itself. Juggle as many ventures as you can, take up new hobbies, join new classes. One of them could be the gateway to your lucky break.

Avoid idleness. This will lead you nowhere. How can you expect to succeed if you wait for the opportunities to come to you, when you can just as easily go out and search for them yourself? Follow your curiosity and let it guide you. Engage in projects you like and keep trying until you get your lucky break. Remember, in Gunther's view, luck clearly is not a blessing sent from above; it's the product of hard work and time spent. If you're busy, eventually you'll run into something that you'd deem lucky.

Find A Destiny Partner

A destiny partner is someone who changes your luck over a period of time.

This is not necessarily a romantic partner and is usually someone just found by blind luck, though it can help if you are actively looking. Maybe it's someone you talk your ideas through that inspires you to do better things, maybe it's someone who always seems to lead good opportunities your way. There are people that can change the course of your life and the nature of your luck, and you often you can do the same to them. Destiny pairs can cause an explosion of good luck when they work together.

Some people are just naturally average by themselves, able to achieve, but struggling to do so. Sometimes, all it takes to become incredible is the company of the right partner. This person can be a spouse, business partner, colleague, or friend. Meeting them happens by chance, so pay attention to your gut. Your destiny pair will elicit a quick, strong, and positive reaction, and good things will begin to unfurl.

Each of Gunther's 13 steps has the potential to change your life. A lot of the time, luck is out of your hands, but with these strategic planning techniques, you have the ability to control as much as you can. It is your attitude and your willingness to achieve that is the sole difference between waiting for life to give you what you desire, or going out there and hunting down success on your own.

Chapter 8. What About *Bad* Luck?

Good luck, bad luck, the worst of luck, struck by bad luck, or on a lucky streak — it seems our world is filled with the idea of luck and its effects on our lives. If you have good luck, then your life is filled with positive events and lucky situations. However, if you have bad luck, then your life can be filled with the opposite.

What is bad luck and how do we avoid it? Is there a way to be better at good luck? Or is it more important to simply escape the clutches of bad luck?

We've talked throughout this book about how to achieve good luck and move closer to situations we might deem "lucky." These include things such as being more open, learning humility so you can put yourself into situations where you might fail, and even simply trusting your gut instinct.

But that's not quite the same as avoiding bad luck. Are you one of those people who are always suffering setbacks? Does everything always go wrong? Could the universe be trying to bring you down? Now we're talking.

Let me let you in on a bit of a secret: Your luck is no worse — and no better — than anyone else's. It just *feels* that way.

Attention

It all begins with what you believe. Have you ever had an event or situation coming up and you were completely petrified of what was going to happen? You might have spent hours and hours going over every single detail, all the possibilities that could go wrong, and a lot of time dwelling on the negatives. Unfortunately, when the big day arrives, things went exactly as you had expected and everything turned into a big disaster.

Sound familiar? Well this may be partly due to your thought process to begin with.

Whatever you pay attention to will grow in your mind.

This isn't a big secret. Even if I tell you not to think of something, you are immediately going to fixate on it. Whenever I think about my favorite ice cream, the craving just grows stronger and stronger until it's all I can think about. This works for negative thoughts and feelings, as well. If you are constantly focusing on things that are going wrong in your life, especially if you think it's "bad luck" and that it's completely out of your control, it will keep growing in your mind until it seems much worse than it really is.

In only a few moments, you could quite easily convince yourself that everything in the world is against you, and you will start noticing more and more instances where this appears to be the case. Maybe you hit every red light on the way to work, or maybe you've broken your fourth dinner plate of the week. When you cast these things in a negative light and blame them on "bad luck," you will almost certainly stop trying because you are so convinced that nothing you can do will improve your prospects.

This fatalism feeds on itself until you find yourself thinking you're nothing more than a "victim" of life's blows, but that just isn't the case. After all, giving up is the only sure path to failure. More often than not, the "losers" and "victims" in life are those who are convinced they will fail before they even start. These people are so sure that their "bad luck" will ruin their chances that they don't even bother to take a chance in the first place. They will rarely accept that the true reasons for their failure have more to do with ignorance, laziness, lack of skill, lack of forethought, or just plain foolishness. These can be hard truths to accept because they are all things that can be corrected, meaning that "bad luck" would no longer act as the scapegoat it almost always is.

If you want to stop blaming luck for all your failures, then you need to take control of your thoughts. They're not helping you be luckier, and they are actively making you unhappy.

Your attention is entirely under your control. If you find yourself beginning to think on only the negatives, stop your thoughts before they can continue further. Send your thoughts to where you want them to go. Stop dwelling on negativity and all the things that may happen. Starve the negative thoughts until they die. The first step is almost always to stop voicing complaints and negativity, because by doing so, you starve them of your mental attention and they more easily forgotten as a passing thought.

The Self-Fulfilling Prophecy

Extending on the previous point is the idea of the self-fulfilling prophecy.

Robert K. Merton, a 20th-century sociologist, may have coined this term, but examples of this can be found in literature as far back as ancient Greece and ancient India. The self-fulfilling prophecy is a prediction that directly or indirectly causes itself to become true due to positive feedback between belief and behavior.

Put simply, this is the idea that a positive or negative prophecy, strongly held belief, or delusion can sufficiently influence people so that their reactions ultimately fulfill the prophecy itself. The classic story of Oedipus, for example, wherein a father had a prophecy that his son was going to kill him, sent him away to prevent it, but the sending away resulted in the very series of actions that led to his death.

This leads to the *behavioral confirmation event*, in which behaviors that are influenced by expectations cause those very expectations to come true. If you think about it, this isn't a hard idea to grasp. If someone expects something of you, whether it be good or bad, more often than not you will live up to that expectation. If you believe you have bad luck, you will act in a way that will ensure bad luck will enter your life, and so on. You create the cycle in which you live through the power of your thoughts and intentions.

I can still remember my very first work presentation that I had to deliver to a group of colleagues about some research I had done. Logically, I knew that my work was fine and that all my data was correct. However, this wasn't as easy to convince myself of in practice. I was so certain that I would forget a point or speak too quietly and make a complete fool of myself. On the day, I found myself trying to do the complete opposite. This resulted into a speech that was mostly yelled, far too long, and excruciatingly slow. I looked and sounded insane. This is a perfect example of how a belief, particularly a negative one, can focus someone's attention and cause the very thing they feared to begin with.

In the case of luck, if you believe you have bad luck, you will ignore every positive thing that occurs and focus blindly on everything that is negative. This is something we all do. You may have had a perfectly ordinary day at work, but as soon as you make one error, it suddenly feels like your whole day starts to turn into a disaster. Often, this is because focusing on the negatives will cause you to act in a way that is contrary to what generates good luck. Instead of being open-minded and willing to explore new possibilities, you let tunnel vision take over and your fear shuts you down.

Bad luck isn't always centered on an event or situation. Plenty of people are certain that they have a particular object that is the sole reason behind every incident of "bad luck" in their lives. Perhaps it's a pair of socks (or absence thereof) that you just know is behind all your troubles, or a song that is always playing when you have a particularly embarrassing moment. Whatever it is, if you believe something will give or bring you bad luck, you will undoubtedly begin to act differently around it, fixate on it in an unhealthy way, and ultimately act differently than you normally would. It is because you act differently and out of your normal flow or behavior that things may seem to just fall apart, just like an athlete who overthinks his game strategy and ends up ruining it all.

If you believe you have great luck, you are more likely to create it — not out of thin air, but by not driving away beneficial situations.

Expectations

As we've discussed, belief can greatly influence the outcome of a scenario.

Expectations are another way of generally looking at the concept of luck. When a certain outcome exceeds your expectations, it is called a good luck manifestation, as things are better that what you had originally believed. Conversely, bad luck manifestations are when certain outcomes do not meet or live up to your expectations. However, both of these rely heavily on these expectations being reasonable and rational. When these expectations become unbalanced or unrealistic, then the results will never be able to meet them.

Let's say you're working your everyday job with your typical salary and you don't expect any additional income. If you come into some extra money all of a sudden, it will seem like good luck. However, if you expect that a stork will drop a large bag full of money into your backyard every day, and suddenly you only receive a small bag, you'd say that you were struck by bad luck, regardless of the fact that the stork had still given you a bag of money.

This is all about expectation. People too often believe that every positive thing that occurs to them is "good luck" and every negative thing is "bad luck." In reality, luck has nothing to do with it, and this is a good thing. Because our expectations so heavily influence our outcomes, if we manage our expectations, then we can manage our luck.

But how can you change your expectations?

This isn't as tricky as it seems, and there are several simple things you can do to help shape your expectations.

The first is planning for the unexpected. By doing this, you can lower your expected outcome because you've already considered that a problem may arise, and can thus increase your luck. Simple things like keeping some emergency money aside for a rainy day can be all it takes to deflect your bad luck. So if you're hit with a broken boiler or are involved in a car accident, you don't expect your car to be in great shape, so none of this is below your expectation and none of this is "bad luck."

The next step is to stop looking for patterns. Chaos and luck don't work in patterns.

It's human nature to place faith in patterns and consistency, but in the case of luck, patterns are your downfall. If you're struck by three instances of good luck, you will consider yourself lucky. Similarly, if you experience three cases of bad luck, you will consider yourself unlucky. Both of these will have unwanted consequences. In the first case, too much "good luck" may cause you to be reckless, as you believe that you're too lucky to experience any hardships, but soon enough you will and you could be completely unprepared for the consequences. Alternatively, too much "bad luck" could cause you to become depressed and lose hope, when just a bit of persistence could be the key to breaking the pattern.

Another thing to consider is *reasonable* expectations. If your expectations are reasonable, probability theory says that there will be manifestations of both good and bad luck. This means that when you manage your expectations, by the rules of probability, you are equally as likely to experience good luck as you are to experience the reverse. If you have understood this concept, then you can split your expectations. Don't always assume that things will go a certain direction. By splitting your expectations and preparing yourself for multiple possibilities, then you can control how these outcomes will affect you.

And finally, there is coincidence. Bad luck is too often confused with coincidence, which is mathematically far more common than you might expect. If there is a possibility of an outcome that you are trying to avoid, whether it's failure or something else, then it cannot be bad luck. This is just normal occurrence. There may have been a 40% chance of failure, but that still means 40 times out of 100, there will be failure. That's not bad luck — it's just real life application of statistics.

There is always the possibility of getting results that may disappoint you, but that's just what it is: a possibility. It's hard to chalk things up to mere coincidence, but sometimes a few consecutive failures will be just that. It's always important to think that no matter the possibility of something happening that will disappoint you, there is always the possibility of the results meeting or exceeding your expectations.

Good luck and bad luck are both equally as probable. It is belief and expectation that are the real culprits in the concept of luck. If you have a positive outlook on a situation and stop dwelling on the negatives, if you have reasonable expectations and plan for any instances where things may go awry, then you may just find yourself with more "good luck" than ever.

That's not to say that you will go out there and nail every job interview or win the lottery; that's mathematically improbable. But the right attitude, outlook and expectation may mean that in whatever situation you find yourself in, your luck is entirely what you make of it — at least you'll be able to avoid what we would consider bad luck.

Chapter 9. Supernatural Thinking

Who among us will openly admit they believe in the supernatural?

People might not willingly admit they believe in ghosts and monsters under the bed, but nonetheless, the vast majority of people have been shown to possess some sort of superstitious routines, have experienced an inexplicable hallucination, or have seen things they can only explain as *magic*.

Want your favorite sports team to win? You might just feel better if you wear the same pair of socks you wore the last time they won.

These things creep into our lives in small, almost imperceptible ways that make it second nature for us to believe in them.

Essentially, *the supernatural* has become a catch-all umbrella term for things which lack a conventional explanation. Can't explain it? Must be something supernatural. There may not always be a clear explanation, but blaming the missing cookies on a ghost and not the dog belies a very interesting tendency for humans to try to apply understanding to that which is out of their grasp.

You've likely read about this tendency when learning about ancient and not-so-ancient civilizations. The Greeks assigned a god to nearly everything as a scapegoat or savior while Native Americans engaged in rain dances to help their crops flourish for the coming harvest. We have the overwhelming desire to feel in control; if we are out of control, then we risk feeling insignificant or subject to danger. When we feel we have control over something, we are suddenly more engaged and invested; if we feel there is no control, we feel helpless to the powers that be.

We believe in supernatural forces exerting control because something we don't understand, yet can blame, is far more comforting than no explanation at all. Humans just don't like to feel that we are random molecules of carbon and hydrogen that happened to coalesce and form somehow — we might be, but it sure feels better if we have a purpose.

Superstitions

Superstitions are the first way we trend to put our faith into the supernatural.

Specifically, superstitions are behaviors or thought patterns that people engage in because they believe in a cause-and-effect relationship. You engage in superstitious acts because you believe it will get you closer to a specific outcome. For instance, if you notice that your favorite football team has won the past three times you've worn red underwear, a new superstition will be born: red underwear only on game days. You might not affect the game itself, but it appears that there is a pattern of causation, so you're going to adhere to it — sometimes even subconsciously.

Classical conditioning is the cause for many superstitions we hold throughout our lives. We commit an act, we see an outcome, and we begin to link the two, even though it's no more than a correlation or simple coincidence. Surprisingly to some sports fans, sitting in the same chair while watching matches likely does not affect the end outcome just because it happened twice three years ago. This is why people don't walk under ladders— because negative occurrences have coincided with that event — never mind the fact that walking under a ladder puts you directly into the path of falling debris.

Yet these beliefs are what humans have a tendency to cling to — and pigeons, as the famous psychologist B.F. Skinner proved in 1948. During his study, he found pigeons learned to continue behaviors that coincided with food appearing, despite the food appearing at set intervals. In other words, pigeons saw patterns that produced an outcome they wanted and kept doing it, even though there was no causal relationship.

Shana Wilson from Kent State University investigated why people, specifically sports fans, engage in superstitious behavior. They concluded that people who engage in superstitious behaviors are more susceptible to what is called the *uncertainty hypothesis*, which is the idea that when people experience a complete lack of certainty, they seek to find a way in which they can exert some degree of control over it. A lack of certainty is extremely uncomfortable, and being able to point to something as a cause eases the underlying tension.

We can find examples of this in our own daily lives. We all hate bumper to bumper traffic. We enjoy driving unimpeded to our destinations. Which would you prefer: bumper to bumper traffic, or driving unimpeded, both of which would culminate in you driving the same distance over the same amount of time? Most of us would choose the latter; we would choose to drive unimpeded because we can control the speed of our car and how slowly or quickly we go. To be stuck in a situation like bumper to bumper traffic where we have zero control and are subject to the infernal gods of traffic — that gives us feelings of hopelessness and helplessness.

Not having control over situations, at the extreme end of the spectrum, is a feeling which underlies certain types of anxiety and depression. What motivation could you possibly have if you were certain everything would turn out terribly, despite your efforts? Therefore, many times, the more important an uncontrollable situation is, the more likely people are to try to exert a measure of control over it through superstitious behavior.

Daniel Wann (2013) discovered that sports fans actually felt they could influence outcomes of games and matches with their superstitious behaviors, which typically involved clothing, food and drink, and good luck charms. Sports fan or not, the more you feel that your life is determined by factors outside your control, this research would argue, the more likely you'll become superstitious.

Superstitions are generally harmless, unless they replace actual work and effort. Problems arise when people can't distinguish between an outcome they can control and an outcome that is beyond their control. Stuart Vyse, author and professor at Connecticut College, chalks superstitious behaviors up to the comforts of illusory control, saying, "There is evidence that positive, luck-enhancing superstitions provide a psychological benefit that can improve skilled performance. There is anxiety associated with the kinds of events that bring out superstition. The absence of control over an important outcome creates anxiety. So, even when we know on a rational level that there is no magic, superstitions can be maintained by their emotional benefit. Furthermore, once you know that a superstition applies, people don't want to tempt fate by not employing it."

Positive superstitions can improve confidence and reduce anxiety because they are the panacea to all that ails you. If you are shy about a job interview and you always wear lucky socks during job interviews, you are going in with a head full of confidence because you feel you are complete and fully armored for battle. This is positive and can be helpful in providing a psychological advantage over not having any superstitious behaviors at all. These help us complete the self-fulfilling prophecy where if we think that we are (because of a superstitious behavior, anyway), then we are.

It's the same belief that can make us proclaim, "The talent was in you all along!"

Superstitions are extremely easy to acquire, and they are likely more widespread than you realize. Our brains are fooling us into a sense of illusory control because it feels more comfortable that way. However, that comfort sometimes distorts reality in very detrimental ways.

Magic

Ah, magic—not the type that magicians peddle on sidewalks, but rather the belief in the paranormal and the extraordinary.

This is something maybe even fewer of us would admit to believing in as adults, but children have been found to accept magic and the paranormal as readily as science and the feeling that their father is the strongest man in the world. Children's brains are sponges for information. They absorb everything and have no sense of filtering for truth, falsehoods, or the fantastical.

Thus, children accept magic as part of their worldview because they don't understand the world well enough to dispel it. At some point, most people lose their belief in Santa Claus for this very reason. The math doesn't measure up for an obese man whipping a set of flying reindeer across the world, descending through every chimney with gifts and enough time left over to kick his feet up and enjoy a snack of milk and cookies. It's close, but it doesn't quite seem possible, and many children can realize this as they grow older. Many things just don't hold up to increased scrutiny as children grow up and experience more of the world and the boundaries of reality.

However, this doesn't mean our sense of magic and the paranormal are completely dashed from our lives — Eugene Subbotsky of Lancaster University believes the belief in magic persists in the subconscious minds of adults even while they consciously reject it.

In other words, they'll never admit to it, but they'll secretly hope to catch the obese man dressed in a red suit on their rooftop during Christmas Eve. They feel, logically, that they shouldn't believe in magic, and logically they should seek alternate explanations for what they may have heard of or witnessed. However, at the slightest chance of magic, they revert back to what is referred to as "magical thinking" — a self-explanatory term. Adults are more likely to rule out *magic* as an option right off the bat and will instead seek all other alternate explanations before resorting to a paranormal option.

This mirrors what we see in everyday life. Adults, for the most part, are conditioned to swear off magical thinking because it can denote a lack of logic, evidence, and even intelligence. Indeed, it is seen as a crutch to simply explain anomalies away as magic, a ghost, or a monster with a hammer.

Magical thinking, however, arises in large part for the same reason superstitions take hold in people's minds: Being able to blame a boogeyman or credit a savior gives us a sense of control over the world and how we navigate it. If we can blame the rain on a mischievous deity, this is more comforting than a total lack of understanding of rain's origins. It gives us comfort in uncertain times and allows us to remain mentally strong.

Giora Keinan of Tel Aviv University found that those who had the highest levels of magical thinking were also those with the highest levels of stress. It is clear then that magical thinking, whether superstitious or in the belief of salvation, is used as a defense mechanism to protect people's psyches against reality. Indeed, in Israel, citizens were subject to constant missile attacks at the time of the study. Magical thoughts can make a person feel that they will be okay.

Someone without magical thinking in an extremely dangerous situation will be too beholden to logic to feel okay. They'll calculate the odds of survival or happiness and see that probability is not on their side. Someone with magical thinking can easily thrive in such a position because they possess one of the most important human traits: *hope*. Magical thinking bestows a feeling of hope and that things will turn out all right.

Jennifer Whitson at the University of Texas conducted additional research into the notion that magical thinking is a type of mental shield from the harsh truths of the world. If something negative has happened, it was for a reason, or there was a greater purpose behind it. That's the type of magical thinking which can allow people to mourn more effectively or work through tragedy. Adam Waytz of

Northwestern University gives meaning to spirits and ghouls we imagine are haunting us: "We create beliefs in ghosts, because we don't like believing that the universe is random."

We've established that magical thinking serves to protect us in many ways, but why are there so many different levels of acceptance of magical thinking?

Some people frequently get their palms read and avoid black cats like the plague, while others choose to live on the 13th floor of buildings because they like the number. What accounts for this difference? Research from the University of Helsinki showed that people with greater degrees of magical thinking tended to interpret random moving shapes as being anthropomorphized or having some sort of intent or purpose. Some said the random shapes were playing tag, while people who had low degrees of magical thinking simply saw random shapes moving in tandem. Those with greater degrees of magical thinking also saw hidden faces in photos with where no such faces were present.

In other words, participants saw what they wanted to see.

People with lower degrees of magical thinking seem to be more adept at seeing random data and patterns for what they are, whereas magical thinking is a lens people will look through to interpret their world. A believer in the paranormal will see fate and kismet, where a more skeptical person will see a simple coincidence. A believer in magic will attribute it to unseen forces, where the skeptic will talk about the small world effect. And so on.

This isn't to say a belief in magic and the paranormal is negative or unhelpful. It's merely to suggest the genesis of a belief in Santa Claus and the sun being one of the wheels of Apollo's golden chariot arose out of a need for self-defense, feelings of control, and a desire to be significant and purposeful. It wasn't necessarily because people engaged in illogical thought patterns — they were just doing the best with the information they had.

Just like with superstitions, beliefs in magic and the paranormal can also be positive because they lend confidence to uncertain situations. If someone holds the belief that they fight well in battle during full moons and their next battle happens to fall on a full moon, they will be ready for action.

Finally, information out of the University of Toulouse concluded that there were indeed certain "cognitive thinking styles" which predicted magical thinking and line up neatly with the other assertions made in this chapter. The researchers delineated two different cognitive thinking styles: intuitive and reflective. Intuitive thinkers go with their gut as quickly as possible, whereas reflective thinkers tend to absorb information and then process it more slowly. In a sense, reflective thinkers are suspicious of their first instincts. Guess which one was more predictive of magical thinking?

Let's imagine the following scenario: You are walking next to a cemetery at midnight and there is a man in a red leather jacket staggering toward you. He appears to be covered in dirt and mold.

The intuitive thinker will immediately jump to conclusions and come up with the first explanation — clearly, a zombie is approaching. This same thought might cross the reflective thinker's mind as well, but they will suppress it in favor of an explanation that takes into account many more factors. This usually results in decidedly *unmagical* thinking.

Superstitions and magic can be seen as flaws in human thinking, but they can also be seen as features in that they act to protect the self. There is no doubt they can occasionally (or often) distort our views of the world, but on the whole, they appear to contribute to mental health and wellbeing. After all, I know I wouldn't feel comfortable wearing a former serial killer's cardigan no matter how many times it had been laundered. This gut feeling, this hunch from extraordinary beliefs, is what guides many of our daily actions.

Chapter 10. Luck in Science

At this point in the book, a few things may have become apparent.

First, things like black cats and walking under ladders don't necessarily impart bad luck. But they do assist in creating negative outcomes for us if we believe that they will. In a sense, we are setting ourselves up for a lack of luck and success. On the flip-side, a good lucky charm does not necessarily imbue one with good luck — it rather makes you feel more invincible, which creates conditions for what we might call lucky situations.

This chapter takes a closer look at something that has happened for hundreds of years, and which can only be explained by the factors and traits of luck we've covered earlier in the book. It's the presence of luck, serendipity, and coincidence — whatever angle you want to take — in scientific discovery.

Many notable inventions or discoveries or conclusions came about not because they were intended, but as a byproduct of something else. People were "lucky" enough to take notice, follow their instincts, and feel open-minded enough to investigate, which led them to take advantage of what was right in front of their faces. Sound familiar? So it's not necessarily that people who tended to make discovery after discovery were luckier or even smarter than others – they simply possessed many of the tendencies we've discussed throughout this book.

There are many instances of luck in the field of science, from the notion that an apple fell onto Isaac Newton's head, prompting him to investigate the concept of gravity, to the invention of Viagra, which was originally supposed to be a heart medication.

The case study I want to focus on is the development and subsequent discovery of *lysergic acid diethylamide*, otherwise known as the psychedelic drug LSD. The discovery of LSD may be of dubious utility to most, but the point is that it demonstrates a path that took extreme openness and curiosity to fulfill.

LSD was discovered by Albert Hoffman in 1943, but it was the result of years of a zig-zag path that began with the intent to create a medical compound to combat ergot, a fungus which was responsible for thousands of deaths as a result of tainted food stores. In the year 857, ergot was theorized to be responsible for an immense plague that came to be known as St. Anthony's Fire. Needless to say, decades of research against the effects of ergot had been conducted — how to reduce it, neutralize it, and deal with the ensuing symptoms.

Hoffman was originally piggybacking on the work of fellow researcher Arthur Stoll's initiatives, whose biggest accomplishment was to break down ergot into two distinct compounds: ergatomine and ergobasine. Following this research, Hoffman experimented with lysergic acid and ergot, and ended up producing a compound which he called LSD-25. As with any new compound, it was tested for medical properties, and there were none apparent except "*the experimental animals became restless during the narcosis.*" Ultimately, the researchers went on to say, "The new substance, however, aroused no special interest in our pharmacologists and physicians; testing was therefore discontinued."

After LSD-25 sat in the dark for roughly five years, Hoffman admitted that he never forgot about it and had always had a certain fixation and curiosity about it. He always remembered the way those animals reacted when exposed to it, and thought there was something special on his hands. This led to Hoffman creating LSD-25 again in 1943 and conducting experiments on it.

However, his experiments and trials did not go exactly to plan. In fact, he became his first test subject inadvertently. One day while at work in his lab with close exposure to the substance, he suddenly felt so mentally uncomfortable he had to go home for the day.

Here's what he wrote in his diary about the experience:

"I was forced to interrupt my work in the laboratory in the middle of the afternoon and proceed home, being affected by a remarkable restlessness, combined with a slight dizziness. At home I lay down and sank into a not unpleasant intoxicated-like condition, characterized by an extremely stimulated imagination. In a dream-like state, with eyes closed (I found the daylight to be unpleasantly glaring), I perceived an uninterrupted steam of fantastic pictures, extraordinary shapes with intense, kaleidoscopic play of colors."

When he returned back to work, he naturally attempted to discover what had caused such an odd reaction. It must have been something in the lab, and he concluded he had likely ingested a small amount of LSD-25, likely through his fingertips. For such a small amount to cause such a massive reaction was startling, and he decided to engage in further self-experimentation to investigate the symptoms further.

Now that his intuition about LSD was showing tantalizing signs of proving justified, Hofmann decided there was only one course of action: self-experimentation. He later wrote more about his fortuitous afternoon exposure to LSD-25:

"Here the notes in my laboratory journal cease. I was able to write the last words only with great effort. By now it was already clear to me that LSD had been the cause of the remarkable experience of the previous Friday, for the altered perceptions were of the same type as before, only much more intense. I had to struggle to speak intelligibly. I asked my laboratory assistant, who was informed of the self-experiment, to escort me home. We went by bicycle, no automobile being available

because of wartime restrictions on their use. On the way home, my condition began to assume threatening forms. Everything in my field of vision wavered and was distorted as if seen in a curved mirror. I also had the sensation of being unable to move from the spot. Nevertheless, my assistant later told me that we had traveled very rapidly. Finally, we arrived at home safe and sound, and I was just barely capable of asking my companion to summon our family doctor and request milk from the neighbors.

The dizziness and sensation of fainting became so strong at times that I could no longer hold myself erect, and had to lie down on a sofa. My surroundings had now transformed themselves in more terrifying ways. Everything in the room spun around, and the familiar objects and pieces of furniture assumed grotesque, threatening forms. They were in continuous motion, animated, as if driven by an inner restlessness. The lady next door, whom I scarcely recognized, brought me milk — in the course of the evening I drank more than two liters. She was no longer Mrs. R., but rather a malevolent, insidious witch with a colored mask."

Hoffman began testing the substance on animals, and he noted that animals had curious reactions similar to his. Mice began moving and walking oddly and licking everything in sight. Cats appeared to be anxious, but with immense amounts of salivation. Chimpanzees were not perceptibly affected to the researchers, but other chimpanzees around the drugged chimpanzees became upset and disgusted, so the drugged chimpanzees were obviously acting in a way extremely foreign to their social norms.

And of course, LSD usage in humans results in similar symptoms. There's a reason is it a noted psychedelic which has been reported to produce hallucinations, voices, and feelings of euphoria.

So how does the curious case of LSD exemplify the presence of luck in scientific discovery? Hoffman approached LSD in a way that all but guaranteed a lucky discovery. Let's take a look at the traits and factors we have discussed in this book.

Openness and curiosity. Hoffman possessed this in spades. It's what caused an idea to lodge in his head for over five years and come to fruition. It wasn't seen as anything productive at his workplace, so he had to engage in the study of LSD-25 himself. He was open to the possibility that it had novel side effects, and he wasn't stuck on the path of investigating ergot and other compounds drawn from it. He knew what he had seen in the animals, and he want to explore it. He knew he could have been wasting his time, but he was open to that failure.

Low neuroticism. Recall that neuroticism is essentially feeling anxiety at events unfolding out of your control. Neuroticism would cause someone to adhere strictly to a schedule or predetermined goal. Therefore, Hoffman possessed extremely low neuroticism because it allowed him to "go with the flow" and fixate and investigate something that wasn't remotely related to his goals at his workplace in curing the effects of ergot. Someone with high neuroticism would have taken a look at LSD-25's test results and discarded them almost immediately because it wouldn't have contributed to his current goals.

Luck versus planning. Hoffman knew that his was a lucky and fortuitous situation from the start because he had happened to see a curious reaction in animals, and he had happened to ingest a small amount of LSD-25 through his fingertips. None of this was by design. However, he saw a pattern that occurred through luck, and ensured that it would continue to occur through stringent planning and experimentation. He didn't confuse luck for planning. He worked to isolate what happened and designed his experiments in a way to discover as much as possible.

Gut instinct. It may have taken five years, but Hoffman finally followed his gut instinct regarding LSD-25. He just knew there was something different and distinct about the way it affected living organisms. He had his first bit of proof that one innocuous afternoon where he had to go home for the day. The rest is history. He followed what his mind told him to follow, and he was proven correct. He took a small leap of faith based on intuition where others would have ignored that gut instinct.

Bad luck into good. Finally, Hoffman possessed the ability to not get deterred by what some would consider bad luck — when he was involuntarily exposed to LSD and felt the ill effects. For many, this would create an aversion to the substance, and even abandoning the idea. But for him, it just increased his curiosity. Indeed, his exposure was proof that something was powerful enough to not even be perceived and still have quite an effect. In fact, he had isolated a substance from a potentially fatal disease, and come out the other end with something that instead provided intense pleasure. That's the very definition of turning something bad into something good.

This process of discovery illustrates just how some people can be considered lucky, or run of the mill. Hoffman these days is considered lucky for his discovery, but it's only in hindsight. If we were to examine Hoffman in real time, we would simply see someone who possess traits and factors of luck, such as openness and curiosity. Yet imagine someone in his position who possessed none of the above. LSD wouldn't be a household name, as other people wouldn't have been interested enough to investigate.

Again, luck isn't necessarily about fate smiling upon you; it's about the way you perceive the world to create the conditions that will allow luck into your life. Some people inhabit these traits and can be said to be naturally luckier, but they are really just putting themselves in better positions on a daily basis. This applies to the field of scientific discovery and invention as well as our normal, everyday lives.

Conclusion

I never did figure out what kind of luck that man with the dirty lucky charms had, but I suppose it was good enough that he felt compelled to keep wearing them after years of gambling.

Or was he simply made more confident each time he wore them, and it reflected in his gambling tactics and methodology? Therein lies the quandary of lucky thoughts, lucky charms, and the quest for seizing hold of luck. Are you really changing your life, or are you simply open to the possibility of changing your life, which causes the change to actually happen.

Regardless, it's been made clear throughout this book that either will suffice. You can engage in strategic luck planning, or you can hold fast to a belief in supernatural thinking. What's important is that the possibility is grasped and the outcome you want is made visible. Once that's there, everything else tends to fall in line.

Personally, I carry a lucky penny in my pocket most days. At this point, it's mostly out of habit, but the comfort it provides tends to imbue me with strength and confidence. Maybe that's what luck is all about.

Best,
Pete
www.petehollins.com

Summary Guide

Chapter 1. Luck of the Draw

What is luck? It can take many shapes and forms, but it is seeing a force causing things to go well (good luck) or poorly (bad luck). Luck is whatever you think it is, and there are many ways to conceive of it that provide varying degrees of comfort.

Chapter 2. The Illusion of Control

Humans have the need for the illusion of control because the idea of random chaos as the norm is difficult for us to grasp. This need to see patterns, however, can lead us to overrate our abilities and fall prey to biases and fallacies.

Chapter 3. As Seen on Oprah …

This chapter covers two methods as people like talk show host Oprah Winfrey might present them — visualization + affirmations, and the law of attraction. The former has been shown to work, while the latter has not.

Chapter 4. Coincidence and Serendipity

These are not necessarily interchangeable with the concept of luck. If they are positive, we might consider them lucky. Coincidence is an improbable thing occurring, and serendipity is a positive improbable thing occurring. Both of these can be explained in simple ways and through analysis of statistical probabilities.

Chapter 5. Traits for Luck

Richard Wiseman names three personality traits that are generally shown to be conducive to luck — low neuroticism, high openness, and high extroversion. In a sense, these traits put you where the action is and allow you to see opportunities as they make themselves available.

Chapter 6. The Four Factors

Wiseman also names four specific factors, one of which was covered in the previous chapter: openness. The other three factors that tended to be associated with luck are trusting gut instincts and not overthinking, having positive expectations, and being able to see negative circumstances through a perspective of positivity.

Chapter 7. "Strategic Luck Planning"

Max Gunther's strategic luck planning consists of 13 factors that are different from Wiseman's factors and traits, and they are more about the way in which you can live your life to have more positive outcomes we would normally call luck.

Chapter 8. What About Bad Luck?

Bad luck is all in the eye of the beholder. Whatever you fixate attention on tends to grow and become more salient, and this is best typified by the self-fulfilling prophecy. Furthermore, whether you expect something to go poorly, and it doesn't, you have good luck. Whether you expect something to go well, and it doesn't, you have bad luck. It is all relative and created in the mind.

Chapter 9. Supernatural Thinking

Occasionally it is important to engage in supernatural thinking – thoughts of superstitions and magic – to enhance the feeling of control and attribute circumstances to things such as luck.

Chapter 10. Luck in Science

The role of luck in scientific discovery cannot be understated, and the discovery of LSD (yes, the psychedelic drug) is a prime example of how the traits and factors we've described can be parlayed into something huge.

www.ingramcontent.com/pod-product-compliance
Lightning Source LLC
Chambersburg PA
CBHW071205070526
44584CB00019B/2919